Fair H

For Apa

MW00810271

*Protect your business, gain peace of
mind, maintain good tenant relations,
and avoid legal trouble by learning
how to comply with tricky housing
discrimination laws.*

Fair Housing Helper
For Apartment Professionals

First Edition

Ron Leshnower

Hillocrian Creative

FAIR HOUSING HELPER FOR APARTMENT PROFESSIONALS
RON LESHNOWER

Hillocrian Creative LLC
P.O. Box 1248
Melville, NY 11747
www.hillocriancreative.com
info@hillocriancreative.com

ISBN-10: 0-9892911-0-3
ISBN-13: 978-0-9892911-0-1

Printed in the United States of America

Cover and book design by Ron Leshnower

Equal housing opportunity logo courtesy of the U.S. Department of Housing and Urban Development.

First Edition: April 2013

10 9 8 7 6 5 4 3 2 1

For more information about Fair Housing Helper products and updates, visit www.fairhousinghelper.com.

This book was written in loving memory of my great uncle Leo, who passed away less than two weeks before federal law began to protect people with disabilities from housing discrimination. Rather than be limited by a disability, Uncle Leo dedicated his life to pursuing his artistic gift while inspiring family and friends with his intellect, creativity, and caring.

This book was also written with sincere thanks to Hillary, Jacob, and Chloe for their love and encouragement.

About the Author

RON LESHNOWER is the Founder and President of Fair Housing Helper and runs the popular FairHousingBlog.com. He is also the author of *Every Landlord's Property Protection Guide: 10 Ways to Cut Your Risk Now* (Nolo), an Amazon.com #1 multi-category bestseller that can be found in law schools and libraries across the country.

A nationally recognized expert, Ron has been invited to speak on fair housing and related topics in front of audiences of housing professionals across the country. He has been quoted in *The New York Times'* "Real Estate Q&A" column, The Associated Press' "Your Money" series, the New York *Daily News*, *Black Enterprise*, the Real Estate Intelligence Report, Minyanville.com, and the *Landlord Law Report*, among other publications.

In 2008, The New York Times Company's About Group selected Ron as the About.com Guide to Apartment Living / Rental. He has since written hundreds of articles and blog posts offering useful tips, explanations of key industry developments, and insightful commentary on a wide range of topics pertaining to rentals. Ron has also written about real estate for Nolo.com and the National Apartment Association's *Units* Magazine as well as several trade newsletters, and he can be seen guest-blogging for MyNewPlace.com.

Ron earned a B.A. from Yale University and a J.D. from Boston University School of Law. He is admitted to practice law in New York and Massachusetts and is a member of the Authors Guild.

Table of Contents

Introduction

What's Fair Housing?

Fair housing as we know it today was born at the close of the civil rights movement, when President Lyndon Johnson signed the Fair Housing Act (Title VIII of the Civil Rights Act of 1968) into law one week after the assassination of Dr. Martin Luther King, Jr. Since that time, fair housing law has further evolved through amendments, regulations, court and administrative decisions, governmental guidance, and the enactment of related laws, including additional state and local discrimination protections.

As its name implies, fair housing law's purpose is to offer equal opportunity in the sale, rental, and financing of housing. For tenants and prospective tenants, this means having the freedom to make housing choices regardless of race, sex, disability, and other factors. But the law has also attempted to balance its protective aim with the rights and interests of apartment professionals like you.

As you make your way through the Quiz in this book and get more familiar with how fair housing law works, you might start forming your own opinions. For instance, you may have a favorable view of some requirements while finding others to be off the mark. Just as you might believe that some provisions go too far, others would say those provisions don't protect enough people or do so at too great an expense.

This book won't tell you what position you should take on any fair housing issue. Its purpose is to help you comply with one of the most important laws affecting your business, wallet, and reputation.

Fair Housing Helper for Apartment Professionals achieves this goal by presenting what you need to know about fair housing compliance in plain English through an engaging, interactive format that encourages knowledge, participation, and lasting comprehension.

Is This Book for You?

If you're a landlord, property manager, real estate agent, building staff member, or other housing professional who interacts with tenants and prospects on a regular basis, then this book is for you.

Many housing professionals think that because they're not racist or sexist, they have no need for fair housing training. But there's more to fair housing compliance than having the right attitude or generally trying to treat people fairly. Not all the rules are obvious and even people who mean well sometimes find themselves getting into fair housing trouble. Also, keep in mind that you could be held liable if employees violate fair housing law on your watch.

Why Learn About Fair Housing?

Simply put, fair housing compliance is good for business.

Finding out how to comply with tricky fair housing laws will help you avoid costly penalties and legal troubles, not to mention bad press and harm to your good tenant relations.

Knowing your responsibilities—and your rights—under fair housing law allows you to run your business with confidence. You'll feel comfortable creating and enforcing policies that you know are fair and legal, and you won't need to run around scared that you or your staff might violate fair housing laws by saying or doing the wrong thing.

Is There Really Much to Learn?

You might wonder how there could be very much to learn about fair housing. After all, the basic concept behind fair housing—treating people the same—seems straightforward.

It's true that fair housing law basically requires you to treat people the same. But if it were that simple, there wouldn't be much to write about—not to mention, discrimination laws such as the Fair Housing Act wouldn't need to be longer than a page.

Once you start to think about which people must be treated the same, and what exactly "the same" means in different scenarios, it's easy to see the complexities.

Plus, as you'll learn, what you need to do to avoid discrimination charges may not seem obvious, which is why even housing professionals who mean well might need to adjust their behavior or tweak their policies to stay in compliance.

How Fair Housing Helper... Helps

Rather than offering a lengthy textbook-style explanation of the law, Fair Housing Helper teaches you what you need to know by first presenting you with a series of carefully crafted questions and answers to get you thinking and participating.

Because you're not able to draw on knowledge you just gained from reading a passage in the previous pages, there's a good chance you won't be sure of the answers. (Think of the Quiz not as a graded exam but as a learning tool designed especially for you.)

Spend a moment thinking about each question and the issues it poses, and then take your best guess. Turn the page to reveal the answer and then digest the explanations. What you read might confirm what you were thinking. Or perhaps it will surprise you in some way.

Progressing through the Quiz under this three-step process—1) starting with a question, 2) guessing the answer, and 3) absorbing the explanation—will help you learn about key fair housing principles and the reasoning behind them.

Before long, you'll realize you know quite a bit about a topic that's so important to your business. You'll immediately gain the confidence of knowing how to handle common situations with prospects and tenants that could lead to fair housing liability and thousands of dollars in damages.

Plus, there's another way that Fair Housing Helper helps housing professionals like you.

The fact that you've chosen to take the time to complete the Quiz in this book shows that you're truly a professional who takes compliance and legal matters seriously.

Should you need to defend yourself against a fair housing complaint, this small purchase can paint you in a positive light, bolstering your credibility with a judge and helping you avoid costly punitive damages.

Go for the Gold

Complete the Quiz and you've earned your designation as a FairHousingHelper.com Gold Professional. You'll get a badge to include on your Web site and marketing materials and a personalized certificate for your office wall to mark your achievement and display your commitment to fair housing compliance.

Details follow the Quiz in "Next Steps."

Go Beyond the Book

Want to learn more about fair housing and gain greater insight into successful compliance?

Visit one or more online destinations in the family of Fair Housing Helper Web sites:

✓ **FairHousingHelper.com**

>Learn about new products and updates relating to fair housing compliance, special promotions, and more.

✓ **FairHousingResources.com**

>Gain access to the full text of the Fair Housing Act, its regulations, related laws, helpful guidance, and more. You'll also find a handy pull-down menu of additional protected classes by state.

✓ **FairHousingBlog.com**

>Find out how important fair housing issues have played out in real-life situations. Read the true stories of others who learned compliance lessons the hard way so you can avoid similar costly mistakes. Feel free to add to the discussion by sharing your thoughts with a comment.

Quiz

Instructions

This Quiz contains multiple-choice and true-or-false questions covering a wide range of important fair housing topics and concepts.

Read each question carefully and use your best judgment to select an answer. If you need help with the multiple-choice questions, look at the bottom of the page for a hint.

You won't find an answer key at the end of this book. Instead, after you answer a question, turn the page for the correct answer and read the explanations. Then, proceed to the next question.

If you prefer, you may skip around, but don't forget to return to finish the entire Quiz.

Extra Challenge: Come back later to repeat the Quiz until you can answer every question correctly and explain the reasoning behind each answer.

Abbreviations Used in the Quiz

DOJ = U.S. Department of Justice

FHA = Fair Housing Act
(Title VIII of the Civil Rights Act of 1968)

HUD = U.S. Department of Housing and Urban Development

Question #1:

True or false?

Landlords who aren't racist, sexist, or prejudiced in any way won't get into fair housing trouble.

The correct answer to Question #1 is:

False.

Explanation: If you're not racist, sexist, or prejudiced in any way, you're more likely to comply with the FHA, since this law is rooted in principles of social fairness and equality. But simply having these attributes isn't the same thing as knowing how to be in compliance with fair housing laws. Sometimes, even actions taken with good intentions could lead to fair housing violations.

Question #2:

Which of the following is a protected class under the FHA?

a. Color.

b. Source of income.

c. Military status.

d. Age.

Hint: It's closely related
to one of the other seven
protected classes under the FHA.

The correct answer to Question #2 is:

a. Color.

Color is one of the seven so-called protected classes under the FHA. It refers to discrimination based on the color or shade of a person's skin. It's closely related to racial discrimination and is often alleged along with race-based fair housing complaints. But it applies even if a landlord or other housing professional didn't make any decisions based on a prospect's or tenant's race. For instance, favoring light-skinned people over dark-skinned people (even of the same race) would violate this ban.

The seven protected classes under the FHA include race, color, religion, national origin, sex, disability, and familial status. (The FHA was amended by the Housing and Community Development Act on August 22, 1974, to add sex as a protected class, and again by the Fair Housing Amendments Act in 1988, to add disability ("handicap") and familial status as protected classes, effective March 12, 1989. Legislative attempts to add other protected classes to the FHA have so far proven unsuccessful.)

Explanation of Incorrect Answers

b. Source of income.

Source of income is a popular protected class in many states and municipalities, but it's not a protected class under the FHA. This means that unless you live in a state, county, city, or town that protects against discrimination based on source of income, you can't expect federal protection. Key to any tenant screening is checking if an applicant has the ability to pay rent in full and on time. Source of income refers to where tenants get the money they use to pay their rent and other expenses. Although some states also protect people based on public assistance status, source of income has been interpreted to mean landlords can't turn away applicants simply because they have housing choice (Section 8) vouchers.

c. Military status.

Military status (and veteran status) is also commonly found among state and local fair housing laws, but it's also not a protected class under the FHA.

d. Age.

Many people think that federal law protects people against housing discrimination based on age, especially since it's protected in employment. (The Age Discrimination in Employment Act of 1967 [ADEA] protects people who are 40 years of age or older.) States and municipalities that protect people based on their age either don't specify an age, clarify that it applies to people who are at least 18 (for example, Hawaii protects people who are "over the age of majority or emancipated minors"), or list a qualifying age. The qualifying age may be as low as 40 (such as is the case in Illinois and North Dakota) but it can be higher (for example, in Virginia it's 55). Iowa's age protection applies only to visitors. Also, note that although age isn't a protected class under the FHA, families with children under 18 are protected against discrimination under the FHA's ban on familial status discrimination. Landlords may, however, rent some or all of their apartments to tenants over a certain age if they follow one or more of the FHA's senior housing exemptions.

Question #3:

True or false?

It's legal for a landlord to discriminate if the landlord belongs to the class of people being discriminated against.

The correct answer to Question #3 is:

False.

Explanation: Some people think it's okay if a landlord discriminates against a class of people that includes herself. Legally, the race, religion, sex, or other protected class of the landlord is irrelevant in determining FHA violations. So, if a landlord discriminates against families with children, for example, it doesn't matter if the landlord has young children. Or if a landlord requires black applicants to rent apartments on a certain floor, the landlord can't escape liability if she herself is black.

Question #4:

True or false?

It's possible to experience housing discrimination over e-mail.

The correct answer to Question #4 is:

True.

Explanation: Usually, landlords who discriminate do so after meeting a prospect, making decisions based on how the prospect looks or what the landlord surmises about the prospect's background. But it's also possible for a prospect to face discrimination just by e-mailing a landlord to inquire about vacancies. For example, a landlord who ignores an e-mail because the name gives him the impression that the person is Muslim is engaging in "name profiling" and is violating the FHA's ban on discrimination based on religion. Similarly, a landlord who suspects, based on a prospect's grammar, that she was born in another country and decides to lie about vacancies at the building is engaging in "linguistic profiling" and is discriminating based on national origin.

Question #5:

True or false?

Both written statements (such as wording in an apartment ad) and oral statements (such as telephone responses to prospective tenants' questions) could lead to fair housing violations, if discriminatory.

The correct answer to Question #5 is:

True.

Explanation: The medium or manner in which a statement is communicated doesn't affect whether there may be liability for it. If a landlord puts a discriminatory statement in an ad or says something similar to a prospect on the phone, each instance may be considered a fair housing violation.

Question #6:

True or false?

It's smart, as a matter of maintaining good tenant relations, for landlords to ask new tenants if they believe they've been treated in a nondiscriminatory way during the apartment application process, and then periodically poll tenants to see if they believe they're being treated fairly.

The correct answer to Question #6 is:

False.

<u>Explanation:</u> There's no need to ask tenants about your fair housing compliance, and doing so can be self-sabotaging. If you're treating tenants fairly, they'll know it and probably appreciate it. If you've done something to a tenant that's possibly discriminatory but the tenant hasn't brought it to your attention or filed a complaint, querying tenants about your fair housing record is just asking for trouble.

Question #7:

A federal law, the FHA applies to which of the following?

a. All 50 states.

b. All 50 states plus the District of Columbia.

c. All 50 states plus the District of Columbia and the Commonwealth of Puerto Rico.

d. All 50 states plus the District of Columbia, the Commonwealth of Puerto Rico, and the territories and possessions of the United States.

*Hint: The FHA's coverage
is broader than you might think.*

The correct answer to Question #7 is:

d. All 50 states plus the District of Columbia, the Commonwealth of Puerto Rico, and the territories and possessions of the United States.

The FHA's geographic coverage is broad, protecting tenants on all American soil, from the 50 states and District of Columbia to Puerto Rico and all territories and possessions of the United States. HUD's Office of Fair Housing and Equal Opportunity (FHEO), which administers and enforces fair housing laws, maintains ten regional offices and several field offices across the country.

Explanation of Incorrect Answers

a. All 50 states.

b. All 50 states plus the District of Columbia.

c. All 50 states plus the District of Columbia and the Commonwealth of Puerto Rico.

Each one of these options is incorrect because it doesn't include the entire United States.

Question #8:

True or false?

There's no difference between discrimination based on race and color.

The correct answer to Question #8 is:

False.

Explanation: Race and color are two of the FHA's seven protected classes. If they were identical, there would be no need for both of them. Race and color are closely related and fair housing complaints alleging discrimination based on one of these protected classes often involves the other. But landlords and other housing professionals could be accused of discrimination based only on color if they're really making decisions based on an applicant's skin color. Similarly, landlords could run afoul of only racial discrimination if they single out people of certain races for inferior treatment (regardless of the skin color of those people and others).

Question #9:

True or false?

States may not enforce their own fair housing laws if they ban discrimination based on protected classes not included in the FHA.

The correct answer to Question #9 is:

False.

Explanation: Many states and municipalities have their own fair housing laws that ban discrimination based on the same protected classes as the FHA as well as, in many cases, additional protected classes such as military status, source of income, and sexual orientation. If a state, county, city, or town has its own fair housing law, landlords and other housing professionals are responsible for complying with that law as well as with the FHA.

Question #10:

Each one of the following federal agencies is charged with enforcing the FHA except:

a. HUD.

b. The DOJ.

c. The Equal Employment Opportunity Commission.

d. None of the above.

*Hint: The FHA applies only
to housing discrimination.*

The correct answer to Question #10 is:

c. The Equal Employment Opportunity Commission.

The Equal Employment Opportunity Commission (EEOC) is the only federal agency listed that doesn't play a role in policing compliance with the FHA. The EEOC is tasked with investigating and enforcing discrimination in the workplace, not in housing.

Explanation of Incorrect Answers

a. HUD.

HUD is the federal agency charged with primary responsibility for enforcing the FHA. Prospects and tenants who believe they've become the victim of illegal housing discrimination may pursue a claim with HUD (through the agency's Office of Fair Housing and Equal Opportunity [FHEO]) and ultimately have their case heard in front of an administrative law judge.

b. The DOJ.

The DOJ also plays an important role in fair housing enforcement. The FHA authorizes the DOJ to bring lawsuits for suspected engagement in a "pattern or practice" of housing discrimination when a denial of rights to a group raises an issue of general public importance. The DOJ, through its Housing and Civil Enforcement Section of the Civil Rights Division, may also bring lawsuits in federal district court on behalf of alleged victims referred by HUD. If force or threat of force is used to deny or interfere with fair housing rights, then the DOJ, through the Criminal Section of the Civil Rights Division, may institute criminal proceedings.

d. None of the above.

This choice is incorrect because the EEOC (choice c) doesn't play a role in FHA enforcement.

Question #11:

What's the basic structure of fair housing laws in the United States?

a. On the federal level, the FHA applies across the United States. State and local governments cannot adopt their own fair housing laws, as they would automatically conflict with the federal law.

b. On the federal level, the FHA applies across the United States. In addition, states and many local governments have adopted their own fair housing laws that offer greater protections or enforcement options.

c. There is no federal law governing housing discrimination. The FHA refers to a network of laws from participating states.

d. None of the above.

Hint: Fair housing laws exist
at more than just the federal level.

The correct answer to Question #11 is:

b. On the federal level, the FHA applies across the United States. In addition, states and many local governments have adopted their own fair housing laws that offer greater protections or enforcement options.

Since 1968, the core source of fair housing legislation has been the FHA. A federal law that applies across the United States, the FHA protects prospects and tenants based on seven protected classes, including race, color, religion, national origin, sex (added in 1974), disability, and familial status (both added in 1989). In addition to offering protections, the FHA established an enforcement mechanism through which alleged victims may seek relief. In addition to the FHA, most states and many counties, cities, and towns have adopted similar fair housing laws. Very often, they protect prospects and tenants based on additional protected classes, such as source of income, sexual orientation, and age. But even if they mirror the FHA, such state and local fair housing laws offer alleged victims another avenue to pursue justice and seek redress for harm they claim to have suffered.

Explanation of Incorrect Answers

a. On the federal level, the FHA applies across the United States. State and local governments cannot adopt their own fair housing laws, as they would automatically conflict with the federal law.

It's true that the FHA is a federal law that applies across the United States. But state and local governments can—and, in many cases, have— adopted their own fair housing laws that expand protection to prospects and tenants within their jurisdiction. Such laws don't automatically conflict with the FHA.

c. There is no federal law governing housing discrimination. The FHA refers to a network of laws from participating states.

The FHA is the federal law governing housing discrimination. It applies to all states and is separate from any fair housing laws passed on the state level.

d. None of the above.

This choice is incorrect because the FHA applies across the United States, and state and local governments have also adopted their own fair housing laws (choice b).

Question #12:

Which of the following is a way in which a tenἑ
seek justice or compensation under the FHA?

a. A tenant may bring a private lawsuit against the
   landlord.

b. A tenant may request that the federal government
   pursue a claim against the landlord on the tenant's
   behalf.

c. A tenant may request that a fair housing organization
   pursue a claim against the landlord on the tenant's
   behalf.

d. All of the above.

Hint: Many tenants don't realize
the number of options available to
them following alleged FHA violations.

The correct answer to Question #12 is:

d. All of the above.

Tenants (and prospective tenants) who believe they are the victim of illegal housing discrimination have several options available to them to pursue justice, if they so choose. A tenant may bring a private, civil lawsuit against a landlord in federal district court, request that the federal government pursue a claim against the landlord on the tenant's behalf, or request that a fair housing organization pursue a claim against the landlord on the tenant's behalf.

Explanation of Incorrect Answers

a. The tenant may bring a private lawsuit against the landlord.

b. The tenant may request that the federal government pursue a claim against the landlord on the tenant's behalf.

c. The tenant may request that a fair housing organization pursue a claim against the landlord on the tenant's behalf.

Each one of these is a way for a tenant to seek justice and compensation under the FHA, so all of the above (choice d) is correct.

Question #13:

True or false?

Tenants don't need to hire an attorney to pursue a claim under the FHA.

The correct answer to Question #13 is:

True.

<u>Explanation:</u> Not only isn't hiring an attorney required, but it's realistic for many prospects and tenants when it comes to pursuing a claim under the FHA, mainly because of the administrative option available to alleged victims of discrimination. Prospects and tenants who believe they've been discriminated against can file a complaint with HUD at no charge, by phone, online (via www.hud.gov), or even on their smartphone through the agency's app. HUD will investigate their complaint and, if the agency believes it has merit, will pursue it on their behalf.

Question #14:

True or false?

If a tenant believes a landlord discriminated against her and her guest, both she and the guest can file a fair housing complaint against that landlord.

The correct answer to Question #14 is:

True.

Explanation: It's important to realize two points when it comes to tenants' guests. First, guests who believe they're the victims of discrimination can file a fair housing complaint. Second, tenants can file a fair housing complaint if they believe they were discriminated against because of the race, religion, or other protected characteristic of a guest.

Question #15:

Government agencies and fair housing organizations have been known to send "testers" to apartment buildings. Testers pretend to be interested in vacancies but the purpose of their visit is only to check that a landlord's procedures and actions comply with fair housing laws. Which of the following statements is true about testing?

a. It's illegal because it's a process that obtains information through secrecy and trickery.

b. It's only illegal if a government agency does it.

c. It has been proven to be an effective way to get more evidence about a landlord's alleged discrimination.

d. b and c.

Hint: The use of deception doesn't necessarily make a course of action illegal.

The correct answer to Question #15 is:

c. It has been proven to be an effective way to get more evidence about a landlord's alleged discrimination.

Time and again, testing has proven quite effective in bolstering the case of an alleged victim of housing discrimination. Not only has testing often revealed more evidence about a landlord's alleged discriminatory policy, but it has uncovered additional acts for which landlords have been held liable.

Explanation of Incorrect Answers

a. It's illegal because it's a process that obtains information through secrecy and trickery.

The fact that there may be secrecy or trickery involved doesn't make testing illegal. Testers aren't supposed to trick landlords into making illegal statements. Instead, they hide their reason for asking questions, which increases the chances that a landlord, property manager, or other housing professional would answer questions about apartment availability and other topics the way that they normally would.

b. It's only illegal if a government agency does it.

Testing is legal regardless of whether the testers are from a government agency (such as HUD) or a non-profit fair housing organization or other group.

d. b and c.

Testing has been proven to be an effective way to get more evidence about a landlord's alleged discrimination (choice c), but it's not true that it's illegal for government agencies to participate (choice b).

Question #16:

It has been just over a year since an alleged incident of housing discrimination by a landlord against a tenant. The tenant may:

a. File a complaint with HUD or sue the landlord.

b. File a complaint with HUD but not sue the landlord.

c. Sue the landlord but not file a complaint with HUD.

d. File a complaint with the DOJ but not with HUD and not sue the landlord.

Hint: Tenants must act faster if they wish to pursue a fair housing complaint with HUD.

The correct answer to Question #16 is:

c. Sue the landlord but not file a complaint with HUD.

The statute of limitations for filing a fair housing complaint with HUD is one year. However, if you wish to bring a private lawsuit against a landlord or other housing professional, you have up to two years to file a fair housing claim in federal court. States and municipalities that have their own fair housing laws often have similar limitations.

Explanation of Incorrect Answers

a. File a complaint with HUD or sue the landlord.

After a year has passed, it's too late to file a fair housing complaint with HUD. But it's not too late to bring a private lawsuit against a landlord for an alleged fair housing violation.

b. File a complaint with HUD but not sue the landlord.

Filing a complaint with HUD is no longer an option after a year has passed since the alleged discrimination. However, it's not too late to pursue a private claim against a landlord, which must be brought within two years.

d. File a complaint with the DOJ but not with HUD and not sue the landlord.

It's true that it's too late to file a complaint with HUD after a year has passed. However, it's not too late to bring a private lawsuit against a landlord. Also, the DOJ brings fair housing complaints on behalf of prospects and tenants if referred to that agency by HUD.

Question #17:

True or false?

After a tenant files a fair housing complaint with HUD, the agency may interview the landlord and others who witnessed or have information about the alleged discrimination.

The correct answer to Question #17 is:

True.

Explanation: If a tenant who believes she's the victim of housing discrimination files a fair housing complaint with HUD, the agency first will investigate the complaint to determine if it has merit. This may involve talking with the landlord, staff, neighbors, and others who may have observed the alleged discriminatory acts or be able to offer information about it.

Question #18:

True or false?

A civil penalty, injunctive relief, mandatory fair housing training, compensatory damages, damages for emotional distress, attorney's fees, punitive damages, and even imprisonment are all possible consequences of FHA violations.

The correct answer to Question #18 is:

True.

<u>Explanation:</u> Each one of the items listed is a possible consequence of violating the FHA. Punitive damages are reserved for more extreme cases of discrimination, and imprisonment is authorized in situations where a landlord or other housing professional uses intimidation.

Question #19:

If a tenant files a fair housing complaint with HUD, which of the following definitely won't happen?

a. The tenant and landlord will sign a conciliation agreement.

b. A HUD administrative law judge will hear the case.

c. The DOJ will argue the tenant's case in federal court.

d. HUD will charge the landlord with discrimination after issuing a "determination of reasonable cause."

e. HUD will charge the landlord with discrimination after issuing a "determination of no reasonable cause."

f. c and e.

*Hint: HUD needs reasonable cause
to declare that a landlord has discriminated.*

The correct answer to Question #19 is:

e. HUD will charge the landlord with discrimination after issuing a "determination of no reasonable cause."

After investigating an alleged victim's claim of unlawful housing discrimination, HUD will issue a "determination of no reasonable cause" if there's insufficient evidence to proceed. If this happens, then the administrative route ends and HUD doesn't charge the landlord with discrimination.

Explanation of Incorrect Answers

 a. The tenant and landlord will sign a conciliation agreement.

The FHA requires HUD to encourage tenants and landlords to come to terms with each other without a hearing. If successful, then the parties sign a conciliation agreement and HUD closes the case. A party to a conciliation agreement can ask the DOJ to enforce the agreement against a noncompliant party, if applicable.

b. A HUD administrative law judge will hear the case.

If conciliation doesn't work and HUD issues a "determination of reasonable cause" and charge of discrimination, then an impartial judge at HUD, known as an administrative law judge, will hear both sides and decide issues of liability.

c. The DOJ will argue your case in federal court.

As an alternative to a hearing in front of a HUD administrative law judge, a party may, within 20 days of receipt of HUD's charge of discrimination, elect to have the case heard in federal civil court. Within 30 days of such election, the DOJ will file a federal civil action.

d. HUD will charge the landlord with discrimination after issuing a "determination of reasonable cause."

If HUD finds enough evidence to proceed with a fair housing complaint against a landlord and issues a "determination of reasonable cause," it will then charge the landlord with discrimination.

f. c and e.

It's possible the DOJ will argue the tenant's case in federal court if either party elects this option.

Question #20:

True or false?

Landlords may retaliate in limited ways against tenants who bring or threaten to bring fair housing complaints against them.

The correct answer to Question #20 is:

False.

Explanation: The FHA expressly bars landlords from taking measures to retaliate against tenants who bring or even threaten to bring a fair housing complaint against them. Although it may be tempting, landlords can't restrict access to amenities, limit privileges, raise rent or take any other adverse action against a tenant simply because the tenant is pursuing a fair housing claim through proper, legal channels. Keep in mind that coercion or retaliation is a violation of the FHA, and so even if a tenant's claim of landlord discrimination is false or unsuccessful, the landlord may still get into fair housing trouble by acting in retaliation.

Question #21:

Except for when it comes to advertising, the FHA doesn't apply to:

a. Owner-occupied apartment buildings that have four or fewer apartments.

b. Most situations where a single-family house is sold or rented without a broker.

c. All of the above.

d. None of the above.

*Hint: The FHA's protections
don't cover all types of housing.*

The correct answer to Question #21 is:

c. All of the above.

The FHA is widely applicable to multifamily housing. However, in each of the situations listed, the FHA doesn't apply, aside from discriminatory advertising provisions. (Note that state and local fair housing laws may have broader coverage.)

Explanation of Incorrect Answers

a. Owner-occupied apartment buildings that have four or fewer apartments.

If a building doesn't have many apartments in it (under five) and the landlord occupies one of those apartments, then the FHA doesn't apply.

b. Most situations where a single-family house is sold or rented without a broker.

People often use brokers to buy and sell single-family houses, as well as to rent them out to tenants. But owners who try to sell or lease their house without involving brokers in most circumstances aren't subject to the FHA.

d. None of the above.

This answer is incorrect because each one of the above scenarios (choice c) is an example of an exception to the FHA's coverage.

Question #22:

True or false?

Tenants must be under a written lease to enjoy fair housing protections.

The correct answer to Question #22 is:

False.

Explanation: Tenants who don't have a written lease but occupy an apartment under a month-to-month rental agreement are protected by the FHA. Plus, the law also protects prospective tenants, who don't occupy an apartment but are looking to do so.

Question #23:

True or false?

Fair housing laws apply only if a landlord receives federal assistance or participates in an affordable housing program.

The correct answer to Question #23 is:

False.

Explanation: Many people think that housing discrimination laws apply only to affordable housing. But they apply to conventional housing as well, including luxury apartment complexes.

Question #24:

True or false?

Landlords may have more fair housing responsibilities or there may be additional consequences for noncompliance if a landlord participates in affordable housing programs.

The correct answer to Question #24 is:

True.

Explanation: By agreeing to participate in an affordable housing program, landlords may need to take on additional responsibilities or face potentially greater consequences when it comes to fair housing compliance. For example, a HUD rule that took effect on March 5, 2012, imposes a ban on discrimination based on sexual orientation, gender identity, and marital status in HUD housing programs. Also, landlords who participate in the federal low-income housing tax credit program and get fair housing violations put their tax credits at risk.

Question #25:

True or false?

Once a tenant's lease ends and the tenant has moved out of an apartment, the landlord is in the clear as far as fair housing complaints are concerned.

The correct answer to Question #25 is:

False.

Explanation: Once a tenant's lease ends and the tenant has moved out of an apartment, chances are there won't be an opportunity for the tenant to face discrimination from that landlord. But that doesn't meant that the landlord is in the clear as far as possible fair housing complaints are concerned. Landlords who, for whatever reason, have been fearful that a particular tenant might complain to HUD shouldn't breathe a sigh of relief just because the tenant has moved out and hasn't taken action. Tenants may bring fair housing complaints against former landlords, too. People who believe they're the victim of unlawful housing discrimination have up to a year after the alleged discrimination occurs to complain to HUD, or up to two years to file a private lawsuit in federal district court. States and municipalities that have their own fair housing laws may have an even longer statute of limitations period.

Question #26:

If the refrigerators in all the apartments in a building need to be replaced, the landlord should proceed:

a. In random order.

b. In alphabetical order by tenant name.

c. In ascending order of apartment number.

d. Any of the above.

e. None of the above.

Hint: Following a nondiscriminatory order helps you steer clear of fair housing trouble.

The correct answer to Question #26 is:

d. Any of the above.

Each of the choices listed reflects a valid, nondiscriminatory way of getting all the refrigerators in a building replaced.

Explanation of Incorrect Answers

a. In random order.

Proceeding with maintenance and repairs at random is nondiscriminatory because it means the landlord chooses apartments without any criteria.

b. In alphabetical order by tenant name.

c. In ascending order of apartment number.

Replacing appliances either in alphabetical order by tenant name or in ascending order of apartment number are both nondiscriminatory because the only determining factor is a letter or number that bears no relation to a tenant's race, religion, sex, or other protected class.

e. None of the above.

This choice is incorrect because any of the above choices (choice d) would work as a nondiscriminatory way of getting all the refrigerators in a building replaced.

Question #27:

To avoid fair housing violations, landlords shouldn't give priority to:

a. Repairs of issues that pose a health or safety risk to tenants.

b. Repairs of issues that are causing damage.

c. Repairs that are requested by white tenants.

d. All of the above.

*Hint: Landlords who offer
superior customer service to
tenants based on race, religion, or
another protected class run afoul of the FHA.*

The correct answer to Question #27 is:

c. Repairs that are requested by white tenants.

If a landlord is quicker to respond to repair requests when they come from white tenants, such action would be a clear violation of the FHA's ban on racial discrimination. Keep in mind, however, that this is different from saying that a landlord automatically violates the FHA if the repair requests he responds to first are from white tenants. If there is a legitimate, nondiscriminatory reason for responding to certain repair requests first, then the race of the tenants making those requests is irrelevant.

Explanation of Incorrect Answers

a. Repairs of issues that pose a health or safety risk to tenants.

Prioritizing repairs of issues that pose a health or safety risk to tenants isn't discriminatory. On the contrary, responding more quickly to fix problems that may cause injury and lead to liability is smart.

b. Repairs of issues that are causing damage.

If an issue in an apartment is causing damage, such as a leak, it makes sense for a landlord to make prompt repairs. For landlords, keeping the physical structure of the building intact, protecting their investment, and keeping tenants safe are legitimate priorities that don't trigger fair housing concerns.

d. All of the above.

Only the option of prioritizing repair requests by white tenants (choice c) could lead to fair housing problems, and so this choice is incorrect.

Question #28:

True or false?

Landlords can be held liable for the discriminatory conduct of plumbers, electricians, landscapers, and other independent contractors they hire to do work at an apartment community.

The correct answer to Question #28 is:

True.

Explanation: Tenants who claim to suffer discrimination at the hands of an independent contractor often bring a fair housing complaint against both the contractor and the landlord. Often enough, courts have held that the landlord should be held liable, even though the contractor was the only person actually discriminating and was not an employee of the landlord. So, if you hire contractors, it's wise to make sure they're aware of fair housing law and the importance of compliance (for your sake and theirs). You may wish to go so far as to include an indemnification clause in your contractor agreement, so that the contractor will be responsible for court costs, attorney's fees, and any penalty or other damages you're ordered to pay on account of the contractor's alleged discrimination.

Question #29:

True or false?

If prospects or tenants ask a landlord to make exceptions to community rules, the landlord must always refuse or face fair housing violations.

The correct answer to Question #29 is:

False.

Explanation: Landlords can make exceptions to rules as long as they're doing so for legitimate, nondiscriminatory reasons and they're prepared to make the same exceptions for all prospects and tenants who are in the same situation. For example, say you have a rule limiting the use of your building's laundry machines to two loads per tenant per day. If a tenant asks if he can do three loads on a weekday because it's less crowded than on weekends, you don't have to agree. But if you do make an exception, you should amend the rules so that the two-load restriction is limited to the weekend for all tenants. Not only is it okay to make exceptions if done in a fair way, but you might actually face fair housing violations by not making an exception. This occurs if a prospect or tenant needs you to make an exception to a rule as a reasonable accommodation for a disability. A common example is letting a tenant with visual impairments keep a guide dog despite your community's no-pets rule.

Question #30:

True or false?

If a landlord negotiates a lower rent to one tenant, that landlord will need to extend the same deal to all other tenants to avoid fair housing violations.

The correct answer to Question #30 is:

False.

Explanation: Short of any rent limitations, such as ones that may be required by the rules of an affordable housing program, landlords are generally free to set market-rate rents and negotiate at will. If you do agree to a lower rent, you needn't give the lower rent or concession to all current tenants. However, you should be sure that negotiations reflect the current market environment and your business needs and aren't based on discriminatory reasons. For example, if over the course of a HUD investigation of a tenant's fair housing complaint, the agency discovers that the landlord has offered deals only to white apartment applicants over the years, the agency may look into whether the landlord has treated applicants differently based on their race.

Question #31:

True or false?

The FHA bars landlords from refusing to rent to applicants because they have housing choice (Section 8) vouchers.

The correct answer to Question #31 is:

False.

Explanation: Landlords who refuse to rent to applicants because they will be paying some of their rent with the help of housing choice (Section 8) vouchers aren't violating the FHA because the FHA's seven protected classes don't apply. Some state and local fair housing laws, however, aim to protect against this type of discrimination by including source of income as an additional protected class.

Question #32:

True or false?

Landlords can get into trouble for discriminatory statements in print advertisements only.

The correct answer to Question #32 is:

False.

Explanation: The FHA bars discriminatory statements showing a preference for certain types of people to the detriment of a protected class regardless of the medium. So, discriminatory statements that appear in online ads are just as risky for a landlord as those included in print ads.

Question #33:

True or false?

When advertising an apartment community, a landlord should consider the race, sex, and other characteristics of any human models depicted.

The correct answer to Question #33 is:

True.

Explanation: Although repealed, HUD's fair housing advertising regulations caution landlords against using models in ads that don't suggest diversity or openness to renting to tenants regardless of their race, sex, and other protected characteristics. To avoid fair housing violations, a best practice is to aim for both inclusion and equality. For example, a photograph showing only white tenants with black maintenance staff members could give the impression that white people are preferred there.

Question #34:

Which of the following statements in an apartment listing would not clearly violate the FHA?

a. "No families allowed."

b. "No blacks allowed."

c. "Whites preferred."

d. "Neat tenants sought."

Hint: Not all discrimination is illegal.

The correct answer to Question #34 is:

d. "Neat tenants sought."

This statement is the only one that would not clearly violate the FHA, but that's not because it doesn't discriminate. To be sure, "neat tenants sought" discriminates against tenants who tend to keep their home messy in favor of those who like keeping things looking tidy all the time. But housekeeping (or poor housekeeping) isn't a protected class, so this type of discrimination isn't illegal. (A 2002 HUD survey, "How Much Do We Know? Public Awareness of the Nation's Fair Housing Laws" revealed, incidentally, that three out of every four individuals—even those who have a high awareness of fair housing law—incorrectly believed that federal law protects people based on their housekeeping skills.)

Explanation of Incorrect Answers

a. "No families allowed."

This statement would violate the FHA's ban on discrimination based on familial status.

b. "No blacks allowed."

This statement would violate the FHA's ban on discrimination based on race and color.

c. "Whites preferred."

This statement would violate the FHA's ban on discrimination based on race and color. Although the listing doesn't say "Whites only," it expresses a preference for white tenants, which illegally limits prospects' housing choices.

85

Question #35:

Which of the following statements in an apartment listing would clearly violate the FHA?

a. "Ideal for empty nesters."

b. "Perfect for up to three people."

c. "Lower security deposit for applicants with excellent credit."

d. "Come see our new playground."

Hint: Describing an apartment instead of who might be best suited to occupy it is a good way to steer clear of fair housing trouble.

The correct answer to Question #35 is:

a. Ideal for empty nesters.

Advertising an apartment as being ideal for empty nesters implies a preference for renters who don't have any children under 18 living with them, in violation of the FHA's ban on familial status discrimination. This is an example of how describing the types of occupants is risky business. It's always better to describe features of an apartment itself and let prospects decide if an apartment is suited for them.

Explanation of Incorrect Answers

b. "Perfect for up to three people."

Sometimes, landlords limit occupancy to fewer people than an apartment can accommodate because their aim is to exclude families with children. In this case, it's possible that the apartment can really accommodate up to four people, which would mean that this statement has the effect of improperly excluding a couple with two children. But it's also possible three people is the legitimate limit, and in any event, three people isn't so low as to exclude all families with children. So, without knowing anything further, this is not a statement that would clearly violate the FHA.

c. "Lower security deposit for applicants with excellent credit."

Landlords have the right to make valid business decisions to help them find good tenants who will pay the rent in full and on time. Landlords who charge a greater security deposit for applicants without excellent credit do so to help insure against the risk of renting to such applicants (who aren't as financially strong and aren't as likely as applicants with excellent credit to pay the rent in full and on time). Having less than excellent credit isn't a protected class, so requiring a greater security deposit from such applicants isn't a clear violation of the FHA. (In a situation such as this hypothetical one, it's possible that some rejected applicants may argue that charging a greater security deposit for applicants with less than excellent credit amounts to illegal discrimination because the only applicants with excellent credit in the neighborhood are white. Indeed, over the years, courts and agencies enforcing the FHA have held that a rule that's not discriminatory on its face may still run afoul of the FHA if it has a "disparate impact" on a protected class. As HUD clarified in a rule that took effect on March 18, 2013, this generally means that a landlord's policy with a disparate impact nevertheless passes muster under the FHA if it's "necessary to achieve one or more substantial, legitimate, nondiscriminatory interests" and there's no alternative with a "less discriminatory effect.")

d. "Come see our new playground."

The FHA's ban on familial status discrimination means landlords can't discriminate against families with children under 18. A playground is an apartment building feature aimed at families with children under 18, so pointing out a new playground in an apartment listing is fine because it's aimed at attracting—not excluding—families with children.

Question #36:

Which of the following statements should be avoided in apartment advertisements because it will lead to a fair housing violation?

a. "Master bedroom."

b. "Family room."

c. "Walk-in closets."

d. "Great view."

e. None of the above.

Hint: HUD gives landlords leeway when it comes to using common terms to describe available apartments.

The correct answer to Question #36 is:

e. None of the above.

This choice is correct because each of the other listed choices is a statement that HUD has indicated to be facially neutral and not a violation of the FHA.

Explanation of Incorrect Answers

a. "Master bedroom."

HUD has indicated that the use of this statement won't violate the FHA's ban on discrimination based on sex or race.

b. "Family room."

According to HUD, you don't need to worry that using this statement in some ads and not others implies a preference based on familial status.

c. "Walk-in closets."

While it's true that tenants with a mobility impairment may not be able to walk into a "walk-in closet," HUD has indicated that this type of statement that describes an apartment doesn't pose a fair housing issue.

d. "Great view."

It's okay to say that an apartment offers a "great view" even though tenants with a visual impairment may not be able to experience it. As is the case with choice c, above, HUD has okayed the use of such statements that describe an apartment.

Question #37:

True or false?

Even if all tenants in a building are of a certain ethnicity and the landlord believes that the tenants would prefer to keep it that way, it's still illegal for the landlord to give any preference to applicants of that ethnicity.

The correct answer to Question #37 is:

True.

Explanation: The FHA bans discrimination based on race. So, this means that the current tenant racial makeup mustn't play a role by giving landlords an excuse to use race as a factor in future tenant selection. Also, if tenants themselves have a racial preference for future tenants in the building, landlords can't honor such a preference without violating the FHA's ban.

Question #38:

A landlord believes that a prospective tenant won't feel comfortable living in her apartment building because there aren't other families with children living there. Another landlord is afraid that a prospective tenant won't be a good fit with other tenants in the building because they're not of the same race. These landlords should:

a. Try to discourage their prospective tenant from renting in their building.

b. Refuse to rent to their prospective tenant.

c. Start an honest conversation with their prospective tenant to communicate these concerns.

d. Not discuss these concerns with their prospective tenant.

Hint: Some conversations promise to do more harm than good.

The correct answer to Question #38 is:

d. Not discuss these concerns with their prospective tenant.

The best practice when it comes to prospects feeling comfortable with new neighbors is to let prospects decide what's best for them. One family with a child might want very much to live in a building with other children, while another family might not care. Whether it's regarding familial status, race, religion, or any other protected class, landlords should stay out of the business of informing and advising prospects whether to rent based on such considerations.

Explanation of Incorrect Answers

a. Try to discourage their prospective tenant from renting in their building.

Discouraging prospects from renting based on familial status or race is illegal discrimination. The fact that the landlord's motives may appear more benign—in other words, acting out of concern for how prospects would enjoy living among certain neighbors, rather than out of a dislike of children or racism—doesn't make it legal.

b. Refuse to rent to their prospective tenant.

An outright refusal to rent to a prospective tenant based on a landlord's own concerns about their happiness there in connection with their familial status or race is blatant, illegal discrimination. Landlords can only guess whether prospects will be happy living at their building. Prospects have the right to choose to rent an apartment for which they qualify, even if they later regret that decision.

c. Start an honest conversation with their prospective

tenant to communicate these concerns.

Short of discouraging or refusing to rent to prospects, mere discussion of a landlord's familial status or race concerns could also lead to fair housing trouble. A prospect might not share a landlord's concerns, and hearing about the landlord's concerns may give prospects the feeling that they're not as welcome in the building as tenants without children or tenants of a different race.

Question #39:

True or false?

Crime at or near an apartment building can justify the implementation of steering policies that would otherwise violate the FHA. For example, if crime is high in a neighborhood, it's legal for landlords and brokers to discourage families with children from renting apartments in buildings there. Or, if a female tenant in a building recently became the victim of a sexual assault, it's okay for the building's landlord to suggest to female prospective tenants that they look elsewhere.

The correct answer to Question #39 is:

False.

Explanation: A high incidence of crime might very well lead apartment hunters to look elsewhere, but that's for them to decide. Landlords should answer questions about crime truthfully but not go so far as to discourage certain types of people from living at their building.

Question #40:

One morning, a landlord shows a vacancy to a white prospect and enthusiastically points out all the desirable features of the building. Later that day, the landlord shows the vacancy to a black prospect with less enthusiasm. Is the landlord violating the FHA?

a. No, as long as he said the same things to both prospects (regardless of his tone).

b. Yes, if the reason for the landlord's changing level of enthusiasm has to do with each prospect's race.

c. No, as long as he doesn't rent the vacant apartment to the white prospect.

d. Yes, because showing apartments to white prospects more enthusiastically than to black prospects violates the FHA's ban on racial discrimination.

Hint: Behaving differently when interacting with a prospect because of the prospect's race is illegal.

The correct answer to Question #40 is:

b. Yes, if the reason for the landlord's changing level of enthusiasm has to do with each prospect's race.

When it comes to trying to fill vacancies, landlords who put more energy and enthusiasm into making their apartments sound appealing to people of certain races over others are violating the FHA's ban on racial discrimination. It's one thing if a landlord's personality is such that he doesn't act particularly enthusiastic when showing vacancies to anyone. (Such a personality trait may be bad for business, but it's not discriminatory.) It's also not a violation if a landlord uses less enthusiasm with a prospect because of a nondiscriminatory reason, such as because he just learned upsetting news. But if prospects of certain races are met with an attitude or a feeling of disinterest on the part of a landlord, they're likely not to feel as welcome or as encouraged to apply for an apartment and sign a lease.

Explanation of Incorrect Answers

a. No, as long as he said the same things to both prospects (regardless of his tone).

Offering the same information to both prospects is important for avoiding a fair housing violation. But if the landlord speaks less enthusiastically to one prospect because of that prospect's race, then it's illegal discrimination because the prospect's race determines how much the landlord encourages the prospect to sign a lease.

c. No, as long as he doesn't rent the vacant apartment to the white prospect.

If the landlord discouraged the black prospect from renting the vacant apartment because of her race, it's a violation even if the landlord ultimately rents the apartment to someone other than the white prospect.

d. Yes, because showing an apartment to white prospects more enthusiastically than to black prospects violates the FHA's ban on racial discrimination.

A landlord might display more enthusiasm when showing an apartment to one prospect over another for a variety of reasons. The fact that each prospect is of a different race doesn't automatically mean the landlord is violating the FHA. But if the reason for a landlord's greater enthusiasm level when meeting with a white prospect as compared to a black prospect is because of race, then the landlord's actions violate the FHA's ban on racial discrimination.

Question #41:

True or false?

Landlords who don't have at least one minority tenant in each of their buildings are subject to fines under the FHA.

The correct answer to Question #41 is:

False.

Explanation: The FHA doesn't impose an affirmative obligation on landlords to rent to at least one minority tenant in a building. The law requires landlords not to consider race as a factor in tenant selection.

Question #42:

To minimize the chances of a misunderstanding during tenant selection that could lead to fair housing trouble, landlords should:

a. Make sure their set of tenant selection criteria doesn't discriminate against applicants based on a protected class.

b. Put their selection criteria in writing.

c. Give a copy of their selection criteria to all applicants.

d. Update their written selection criteria as their policies and procedures change.

e. All of the above.

Hint: Creating a set of nondiscriminatory criteria and communicating it to all applicants helps avoid violations.

The correct answer to Question #42 is:

e. All of the above.

Prospects who apply for an apartment sometimes get their applications rejected for a reason that surprises them. Too often, this leads them to suspect that discrimination played a role in the tenant screening process. You can prevent unpleasant surprises by reflecting your current screening policies and procedures in a written tenant selection plan. Make sure to give a copy of your tenant selection plan to all applicants so they know what you require and understand that you screen based on legitimate, objective business reasons.

Explanation of Incorrect Answers

a. Make sure their set of tenant selection criteria doesn't discriminate based on a protected class.

b. Put their selection criteria in writing.

c. Give a copy of their selection criteria to all applicants.

d. Update their written selection criteria as their policies and procedures change.

Each one of these is a way in which you can lower the chances of a misunderstanding during tenant selection that could lead to fair housing trouble, so all of the above (choice e) is correct.

Question #43:

Although a landlord is willing to rent to people regardless of their race, which of the following actions could lead to fair housing violations?

a. The landlord discourages minorities from applying.

b. The landlord doesn't bother pointing out all the top selling points of the property to minorities who visit.

c. The landlord tries to convince minority prospects that they wouldn't be a good fit at the property.

d. The landlord assigns minority applicants to a certain floor or section of a building.

e. All of the above.

Hint: Landlords who discriminate in subtle ways may still face FHA violations.

The correct answer to Question #43 is:

e. All of the above.

Landlords can get into fair housing trouble by engaging in a more subtle form of discrimination known as steering. Even if a landlord rents to minority applicants, limiting their choices (such as telling them about vacancies only in a certain section of the building) or discouraging them in any way from renting at the property because of their race (in this case) is illegal racial discrimination.

Explanation of Incorrect Answers

a. The landlord discourages minorities from applying.

b. The landlord doesn't bother pointing out all the top selling points of the property to minorities who visit.

c. The landlord tries to convince minority prospects that they wouldn't be a good fit at the property.

d. The landlord assigns minority applicants to a certain floor or section of a building.

Each one of these is a way in which a landlord can violate the FHA by engaging in steering, so all of the above (choice e) is correct.

Question #44:

True or false?

Steering prospective tenants to rent in a certain part of a building based on a protected class is always illegal.

The correct answer to Question #44 is:

True.

Explanation: Steering may be less overt than actually turning away applicants based on a protected class, but as long as the steering involves taking action based on a protected class, it's illegal under the FHA.

Question #45:

True or false?

To play it safe, landlords should favor minority applicants over white applicants to fill apartment vacancies.

The correct answer to Question #45 is:

False.

Explanation: Many landlords are understandably fearful of becoming the target of a fair housing complaint, especially if they believe that they and their staff members do nothing illegal. Some landlords try to address such fears by favoring minority over white applicants for apartments. However, this type of reverse discrimination actually violates the FHA because it means making decisions based on an applicant's race. If white applicants learn they're being turned away because of their race, they can bring a fair housing complaint. Such a practice can also hurt a landlord's business because it could mean turning away the most qualified applicants because of their race.

Question #46:

True or false?

Landlords who don't include the equal housing opportunity logo (pictured below) and a statement of nondiscrimination in advertising are automatically in violation of the FHA.

The correct answer to Question #46 is:

False.

Explanation: The FHA doesn't require landlords to include the equal housing opportunity logo and a statement of nondiscrimination in their advertising. HUD's fair housing advertising regulations, which were repealed, strongly advise landlords to incorporate the logo and statement in their materials. Many landlords choose to include the logo and statement because it shows prospective tenants that they're professionals who are familiar with discrimination laws and strive to comply. Landlords who don't use the logo and statement aren't automatically violating the law.

Question #47:

True or false?

Landlords may legally discriminate if they believe that not doing so would lead to a fair housing complaint.

The correct answer to Question #47 is:

False.

Explanation: Sometimes, landlords find themselves in a situation in which they're afraid one or even several people will bring a fair housing complaint against them unless they take a certain action. For example, a landlord may be convinced that if she doesn't rent to a certain applicant because of her poor credit, that applicant will insist that the real reason was her religion. But as long as the applicant doesn't meet the landlord's tenant selection criteria and the landlord applies the same criteria to all applicants, the landlord should reject the applicant. If the applicant complains, the landlord will be able to show a consistent policy of following nondiscriminatory criteria. On the other hand, if the landlord makes an exception because of the applicant's religion, then the landlord is actually violating the FHA. Other applicants who were rejected due to poor credit and are not of the same religion could bring a complaint—and win.

Question #48:

True or false?

Landlords may discriminate against prospective tenants if they believe it's in the prospects' best interests.

The correct answer to Question #48 is:

False.

<u>Explanation:</u> Landlords can't decide that people of a certain ethnicity wouldn't feel as much at home in the building, or conclude that the neighborhood is no place for kids since it doesn't offer any parks or other child-friendly features.

Question #49:

How should a landlord or broker respond if prospective tenants ask about the racial or religious composition of an apartment community?

a. They should answer them truthfully, to the best of their knowledge.

b. They should answer them truthfully, after careful research.

c. They shouldn't answer such questions.

d. They shouldn't answer such questions, unless it's clear the person's reason for asking them is to live near other tenants of the same race or religion.

e. They shouldn't answer such questions but direct prospective tenants to Web sites and other resources for more information.

Hint: Conversations about protected classes at an apartment building can easily lead to fair housing trouble.

The correct answer to Question #49 is:

c. Don't answer such questions.

When talking to prospective tenants, be on alert for questions that may solicit information from you about the racial or religious composition of your apartment community. The FHA bans discrimination based on race, color, religion, national origin, and other protected classes. So, engaging in a discussion about your community's racial or religious makeup with prospective tenants means you're helping them make housing decisions based, at least in part, on race or religion, which is illegal. (Note that answering similar questions about other protected classes, such as the number of women compared to men, the presence of children, and the number of tenants with disabilities, will similarly lead to fair housing violations.) If a prospect persists with inappropriate questions, you can point out that fair housing laws prevent you from answering.

Explanation of Incorrect Answers

a. They should answer them truthfully, to the best of their knowledge.

Speaking truthfully is, of course, generally good advice when talking with prospective tenants. But when it comes to the racial or religious composition of your community, it's important to realize that answering such questions, even truthfully and to the best of your knowledge, is problematic because it requires you to act in violation of the FHA.

b. They should answer them truthfully, after careful research.

It's generally a good idea to research a statistic or fact

about your property if you're not sure of an answer before replying to a prospective tenant. But if the question is about the racial or religious composition of your community, then being sure of an answer isn't the only consideration. What's more important is to recognize that such questions are inappropriate (and lead to liability), so you should decline to answer them.

d. They shouldn't answer such questions, unless it's clear the person's reason for asking them is to live near other tenants of the same race or religion.

This answer is incorrect for two reasons. First, it's not always possible to be sure of a person's reason for asking questions about your community's racial or religious composition. More importantly, whether a person's reason for asking such questions is to avoid living near tenants of certain races or religions, or it's to live near others who share their racial or religious background, answering them will put you at risk of fair housing violations.

e. They shouldn't answer such questions but direct prospective tenants to Web sites and other resources for more information.

You might think that declining to answer questions about your community's racial or religious composition while pointing prospective tenants to resources is the perfect compromise. This way, you avoid answering the question directly yet you come across as helpful. Tempting as it may seem, this route is also problematic because you're still helping prospective tenants take race or religion into account when making housing choices. Note that you won't get into trouble simply because a prospective tenant chooses your community after factoring in its racial or religious composition. But helping a prospect in this effort amounts to illegal discrimination.

Question #50:

True or false?

Landlords may set a limit on the number of minority tenants in the building.

The correct answer to Question #50 is:

False.

<u>Explanation:</u> The FHA doesn't require landlords to rent to minority tenants. Instead, the FHA requires landlords not to take race into consideration when evaluating a tenant's apartment application. So, placing a limit on the number of minority tenants in a building would mean turning away qualified applicants based on race once that limit is reached.

Question #51:

True or false?

It's okay for a landlord to choose a tenant out of fear that rejecting the person will lead to a fair housing complaint.

The correct answer to Question #51 is:

False.

Explanation: Landlords should use their own set of legitimate, nondiscriminatory tenant selection criteria to find good tenants for their building who will pay the rent in full and on time. Veering from this, especially if it's driven by fair housing fears, will get a landlord into fair housing trouble. Making an exception to screening policies because of a person's race, religion, sex, or other protected class is, in itself, a fair housing violation.

Question #52:

True or false?

If all tenants in a building are white and a landlord rejects a black prospect's application, the landlord might be violating the FHA.

The correct answer to Question #52 is:

True.

<u>Explanation:</u> Based on the limited information provided, it's not possible to tell if the landlord has violated the FHA by discriminating based on race. The key is whether the landlord rejected the prospect because he's not white. If the landlord rejected the prospect for a legitimate, nondiscriminatory reason, then it's not a fair housing violation—even if all tenants in the building are white.

Question #53:

True or false?

If a leasing agent wants to let co-workers know the race or national origin of a prospect who called or visited, the agent should indicate it with a code on the file or application.

The correct answer to Question #53 is:

False.

Explanation: A leasing agent or other housing professional shouldn't be interested in making sure others know the race or national origin of each prospect. Race and national origin are two of the FHA's seven protected classes, which means making housing decisions based on a prospect's race or national origin is a fair housing violation. The presence of a written race or national origin indication—whether it's comprised of complete words or an internal code—in a housing professional's file implies that race and national origin are factors in the apartment application process.

Question #54:

True or false?

Creating a waiting list to fill apartments as they become vacant will automatically guarantee that a landlord will avoid fair housing trouble.

The correct answer to Question #54 is:

False.

Explanation: Having a waiting list is an excellent idea because it lets you stay in touch with prospective tenants whom you already attracted to your apartment community, and it gives prospects a way to rent an apartment they like once something becomes available. However, waiting lists are filled with potential fair housing traps, and so you should be sure to manage them carefully. Most importantly, when a prospect inquires about an apartment that's not available, don't forget to mention your waiting list and offer to put that prospect's name on it. If you do add a prospect's name to your waiting list, make it clear that the prospect will still need to follow your usual tenant screening procedures at the time he applies. Also, make sure you maintain the list properly so that you select prospects off the list in the order in which they were added.

Question #55:

The FHA's ban on religious discrimination applies:

a. Only to certain "established" religions as outlined in the FHA.

b. Only to certain "established" religions as updated by HUD periodically through notices or regulations.

c. Only to people who associate with a religion.

d. To people who either associate or don't associate with a religion.

*Hint: Statements that
discourage tenants from observing
their religion are in violation of the FHA.*

The correct answer to Question #55 is:

d. To people who either associate or don't associate with a religion.

The FHA very generally and broadly bans discrimination based on religion. There is no requirement that people consider themselves followers of any particular religion in order to gain protection. A landlord who treats a tenant differently because of her religious beliefs or practices can get into fair housing trouble whether that religion is popular or obscure. In addition, tenants who don't associate with a particular religion are protected against discrimination based on any religious beliefs they may—or may not—have.

Explanation of Incorrect Answers

a. Only to certain "established" religions as outlined in the FHA.

b. Only to certain "established" religions as updated by HUD periodically through notices or regulations.

The FHA doesn't list religions nor does HUD provide a list through notices or regulations. The law doesn't apply differently to people who are adherents of so-called established religions. The discrimination ban is about not limiting housing choices for prospects and tenants based on their religious beliefs or practices.

c. Only to people who associate with a religion.

It's not necessary for a prospect or tenant to associate with a religion in order to gain protection under the FHA's ban on religious discrimination. People are protected against discrimination based on their religious choices and expressions, or lack of such choices and expressions.

Question #56:

True or false?

The FHA generally allows a religious organization or private club that owns property to limit occupancy to members or people of that religion, respectively.

The correct answer to Question #56 is:

True.

Explanation: Sometimes, religious organizations and private clubs choose to purchase and maintain an apartment building. As long as the ownership isn't for a commercial purpose, a religious organization may legally limit occupancy or give preferences to people of that religion, provided the religion doesn't discriminate based on race, color, or national origin. Similarly, the FHA lets a private club limit occupancy or give preferences to its members.

Question #57:

True or false?

Prospects and tenants who consider themselves to be atheists or agnostics are protected under the FHA.

The correct answer to Question #57 is:

True.

Explanation: The FHA's inclusion of religion as a protected class doesn't mean that only religious people —or even people claiming to identify with a particular religion—are protected. It means that landlords and other housing professionals can't take religion into account when deciding how they treat prospects and tenants. So, people who consider themselves atheists or agnostics are protected against discrimination.

Question #58:

True or false?

If all the tenants in an apartment building are Christian, the landlord is in violation of the FHA.

The correct answer to Question #58 is:

False.

Explanation: While the FHA bans housing discrimination based on religion, it doesn't penalize landlords who don't have a religiously diverse tenant makeup. The fact that all the tenants in a particular building are Christian is not an automatic fair housing violation. If the reason for this tenant makeup is that the landlord has rejected applications from prospects simply because they weren't Christian, those rejections would put the landlord in violation of the FHA.

Question #59:

When it comes to religious decor in an apartment, a landlord may legally:

a. Require tenants to include certain religious decor.

b. Bar tenants from including religious decor.

c. Pressure tenants to display religious decor.

d. Show disapproval of tenants' religious decor.

e. All of the above.

f. None of the above.

*Hint: Landlords who interfere
with a tenant's exercise of religion
are asking for fair housing trouble.*

The correct answer to Question #59 is:

f. None of the above.

A landlord may not legally take any of the actions listed regarding a tenant's religious decor. Apartment decor is a matter of personal taste, and any decision tenants make when it comes to choosing to include items of religious significance in their own home is protected by the FHA's ban on religious discrimination.

Explanation of Incorrect Answers

a. Require tenants to include certain religious decor.

Landlords can't dictate how religious or observant their tenants should be, which means the decision to display items of religious significance in a tenant's own home is the tenant's to make. Even if a landlord knows that tenants hold certain religious beliefs or identify with a particular established religion, the landlord can't require those tenants to reflect their beliefs in their apartment decor.

b. Bar tenants from including religious decor.

Many tenants like to express their faith by including items of religious significance in their home. Just as a landlord can't require tenants to incorporate faith into apartment decor, a landlord also can't bar tenants from religious displays in their apartment.

c. Pressure tenants to display religious decor.

d. Show disapproval of tenants' religious decor.

These two choices are toned-down versions of choices a and b. Nevertheless, the action they describe is illegal because it means the landlord is trying to influence tenants to take certain action based on religion.

e. All of the above.

This choice is incorrect because none of the choices listed is legal under the FHA (and so choice f is correct).

Question #60:

True or false?

Landlords may legally require tenants who are nearing the end of their lease term to cover religious objects and decor in their apartment to make it "religion-neutral" when showing it to prospective tenants.

The correct answer to Question #60 is:

False.

<u>Explanation:</u> It's a good idea to keep an apartment religion-neutral once it's vacant. Doing otherwise could imply a preference for filling the vacancy with tenants of a certain religion, which would violate the FHA. But landlords mustn't require tenants to cover up or remove religious items in anticipation of showing the apartment to prospects. If prospects visit an apartment that's not yet vacant, they should expect to see an apartment with furniture and decor chosen by its current occupants. Of course, if these prospects become that apartment's next inhabitants, they'll have the chance to personalize it so that it reflects their own taste and, if they so choose, religion.

Question #61:

True or false?

To avoid religious discrimination, landlords should refrain from adorning their common areas with holiday decor such as Christmas trees, Santa Claus, wreaths, and menorahs, and statements such as "Merry Christmas" and "Happy Hanukkah."

The correct answer to Question #61 is:

False.

Explanation: Many landlords and property managers like to decorate the lobby or other parts of their building each year to convey holiday cheer. HUD has clarified that decorating a building with "secularized" terms or symbols (such as the ones listed in the question) to represent the holidays should present no fair housing issues. However, landlords and managers should avoid choosing decorations that convey a deeper religious message or relate more to a religion than to celebrating the holiday season. Also, including religious displays in common areas year-round would lead to fair housing trouble because it gives the impression that the landlord prefers tenants who are religious or associate with a certain religion.

Question #62:

Which one of the following is not an example of discrimination based on national origin?

a. A landlord refuses to rent to someone because he's of Asian descent.

b. A landlord ignores an e-mail request from someone because he appears to have an Asian name.

c. A landlord refuses to rent to someone who is of Asian descent because of poor credit.

d. A landlord refuses to rent to people of Asian descent only if they're not native English speakers.

Hint: The reason behind a landlord's action is important for determining liability.

The correct answer to Question #62 is:

c. A landlord refuses to rent to someone who is of Asian descent because of poor credit.

A prospective tenant who is of Asian descent is protected against discrimination based on national origin. But that doesn't mean that a landlord can't refuse to rent to such a prospect under any circumstances. If a prospect has poor credit, that fact is a legitimate business reason for a landlord to reject the prospect's application (assuming the landlord holds all applicants to the same screening standard). The prospect's national origin would be irrelevant to that determination.

Explanation of Incorrect Answers

a. A landlord refuses to rent to someone because he's of Asian descent.

This is an obvious example of housing discrimination based on national origin. Turning away prospects because of which part of the world they come from is illegal discrimination under the FHA.

b. A landlord ignores an e-mail request from someone because he appears to have an Asian name.

In this situation, the landlord hasn't met the prospect and there is nothing to their relationship other than a single unanswered e-mail. Nevertheless, enough has happened for this to qualify as an example of discrimination based on national origin. As in the situation described in choice a, the landlord here is attempting to limit another person's housing options based on his national origin, which is illegal under the FHA. Note that this type of discrimination, in which a landlord or other housing professional discriminates based on assumptions gleaned from a prospect's name, is commonly known as "name profiling."

d. A landlord refuses to rent to people of Asian descent only if they're not native English speakers.

This is an example of national origin discrimination because a prospect's national origin plays a role here in whether the landlord would consider the prospect's application. If prospects of Asian descent don't meet the landlord's native-English requirement, then it means they can't rent with this landlord (on account of their national origin).

Question #63:

True or false?

Landlords who refuse to rent to tenants who don't have a legal right to be in the United States are automatically violating the FHA.

The correct answer to Question #63 is:

False.

Explanation: The FHA doesn't protect prospects and tenants based on citizenship or immigration status. This means that landlords may require apartment applicants to show that they have a legal right to be in the United States, and that they will have such a right throughout the term of their lease. (For example, a landlord can check that an applicant's student visa won't expire before her lease would.) The key in these situations is to treat all applicants the same, regardless of protected characteristics such as race or national origin, by requiring the same documentation to show evidence of citizenship or eligible immigration status.

Question #64:

True or false?

Some states and municipalities that ban discrimination based on national origin, like the FHA does, also ban discrimination based on ancestry.

The correct answer to Question #64 is:

True.

Explanation: The FHA doesn't define national origin, and so a number of states and municipalities also add ancestry to the list of protected classes in their jurisdiction. This way, they can be sure that it's illegal to discriminate against prospects and tenants based on where they were born as well as where their family comes from.

Question #65:

True or false?

Discrimination based on sex protects only female tenants.

The correct answer to Question #65 is:

False.

Explanation: The FHA's ban on sex discrimination most often involves female victims. But males are protected, too. Also, the sex of the person who is allegedly discriminating is irrelevant.

Question #66:

Landlords may refuse to rent to women under which of
the following scenarios?

a. The tenancy is for a rental house that would require
the tenant to perform a significant amount of manual
labor, such as mowing the lawn or shoveling snow.

b. The current tenant makeup of the apartment building
is nearly all female, and the landlord thinks it's better
for tenants when there's more diversity.

c. The current tenant makeup of the apartment building
is nearly all female, and the landlord is afraid that
this could lead to fair housing trouble.

d. The landlord has had trouble with female tenants in
the past.

e. None of the above, except a landlord may require at
least one male tenant in each apartment.

f. None of the above.

*Hint: Refusing to rent to women
for any reason limits housing
choices based on sex.*

The correct answer to Question #66 is:

f. None of the above.

Sex is one of the seven protected classes under the FHA. So, a landlord can't refuse to rent to a tenant just because she's female under any of the scenarios listed.

Explanation of Incorrect Answers

a. The tenancy is for a rental house that would require the tenant to perform a significant amount of manual labor, such as mowing the lawn or shoveling snow.

Fair housing cases have arisen in which a landlord has turned away a female prospect because there was regular manual labor to be performed and the landlord believed it would be best for a man to handle it all. Whether the landlord isn't comfortable with the idea of a woman taking on tasks that he believes have traditionally been handled by men or he believes he's just protecting women from injury, such a scenario doesn't legally justify turning away prospects just because they're female. In other words, landlords who impose traditional gender roles on tenant selection in their building are violating the FHA's ban on sex discrimination.

b. The current tenant makeup of the apartment building is nearly all female, and the landlord thinks it's better for tenants when there's more diversity.

If the makeup of a building happens to be nearly all female (presumably, through no prior discrimination), landlords can't start turning away qualified female tenants in an attempt to achieve a more gender-balanced representation. Doing so unfairly discriminates against women and violates the FHA's ban on sex discrimination.

c. The current tenant makeup of the apartment building is nearly all female, and the landlord is afraid that this could lead to fair housing trouble.

If a landlord's building is comprised of nearly all female tenants but not because he discriminated against prospects based on sex, then the landlord hasn't violated the FHA. If he lets a fear of possible discrimination complaints lead him to start turning away prospects simply because they're female, he'll then be open to liability for violating the FHA's ban on sex discrimination.

d. The landlord has had trouble with female tenants in the past.

If a particular landlord claims to have had problems with female tenants, his experience can't serve as a justification to turn away qualified prospects in the future because they're female. Doing so amounts to punishing people for the alleged bad acts of others, in the form of a denial of housing based on their sex.

e. None of the above, except a landlord may require at least one male tenant in each apartment.

Requiring that at least one male tenant reside in each household would require a landlord to discrimination against women. For example, it would mean that a single male prospect could rent a studio or one-bedroom apartment, but a single female prospect would need to be turned away only on account of her sex.

Question #67:

True or false?

A landlord can legally require a greater security deposit from female tenants.

The correct answer to Question #67 is:

False.

Explanation: Sex is a protected class under the FHA, so landlords who offer different terms to tenants based on their sex are violating the FHA's ban on sex discrimination.

Question #68:

True or false?

Sexual harassment of tenants by apartment staff may be abhorrent, but it's not a violation of the FHA.

The correct answer to Question #68 is:

False.

<u>Explanation:</u> Sexual harassment of tenants is banned by the FHA because it involves discrimination based on sex, which is a protected class. So, any unwelcome sexual touching or other behavior, such as whistling at tenants or making off-color remarks, offering rent concessions in return for sexual favors, and sending inappropriate e-mails, may lead to fair housing complaints. HUD regulations also make clear that it's illegal to deny or limit "services or facilities in connection with the sale or rental of a dwelling, because a person failed or refused to provide sexual favors."

Question #69:

True or false?

"Familial status" generally refers to the presence of at least one child under 18 in a household.

The correct answer to Question #69 is:

True.

<u>Explanation:</u> Familial status discrimination occurs when a landlord or other housing professional treats a household differently simply because they have children living with them. The term "familial status" refers to the presence of at least one child under 18 years old in an apartment.

Question #70:

To qualify for familial status protection under the FHA, a tenant must be:

a. A child's parent.

b. The legal custodian of a child.

c. The "designee" (with written permission) of the child's parent or legal custodian.

d. Any of the above.

Hint: Familial status protection focuses on the presence of at least one child under 18.

The correct answer to Question #70 is:

d. Any of the above.

If you think familial status protection applies only to situations in which children live with their parents, think again. Familial status protection applies if children live with a parent, legal custodian, or a designee of a parent or legal custodian.

Explanation of Incorrect Answers

a. A child's parent.

b. The legal custodian of a child.

c. The "designee" (with written permission) of the child's parent or legal custodian.

These choices are incorrect because each one isn't the only way a household may qualify for familial status protection under the FHA. Choice d is correct because the adult tenant may be either a child's parent, legal custodian, or designee, which reflects the FHA's broad coverage.

Question #71:

For a household to qualify for familial status protection under the FHA, a child living in the household must be:

a. Under 18 years old.

b. Biological or adopted.

c. Already a household member or expected to be one.

d. Under 18 years old, biological, and already a household member.

e. a, b and c.

Hint: A household with a tenant who's pregnant or in the process of adopting a child is covered under the familial status discrimination ban.

The correct answer to Question #71 is:

e. a, b and c.

The FHA is fairly liberal when it comes to which children qualify a household for familial status protection. Not surprisingly, children must be under 18 years old. However, they may be either biological or adopted. Also, if tenants don't yet have a child living in the apartment but they're expecting a child through pregnancy or adoption, they still qualify for protection.

Explanation of Incorrect Answers

a. Under 18 years old.

b. Biological or adopted.

c. Already a household member or expected to be one.

These choices are incorrect because each one of them is a way in which a child can make a household qualify for protection under the FHA's ban on familial status discrimination.

d. Under 18 years old, biological, and already a household member.

There is no requirement that a parent have biological children. If the only children in a household are adopted, the household also qualifies for familial status protection. Also, it's not necessary that a child already be a household member. A household with a pregnant woman or a household in the process of adopting a child qualifies for familial status protection.

Question #72:

Tenants who are pregnant are protected against discrimination:

a. Only if state or local law includes pregnancy as a protected class.

b. Because the FHA includes pregnancy as a protected class.

c. Under the FHA's ban on discrimination based on familial status.

d. Only if they already have a child.

*Hint: Familial status protection
also applies when a tenant expects
a child to live in the apartment.*

The correct answer to Question #72 is:

c. Under the FHA's ban on discrimination based on familial status.

Although the FHA doesn't include pregnancy as a protected class, the law makes it clear that "[t]he protections afforded against discrimination on the basis of familial status shall apply to any person who is pregnant."

Explanation of Incorrect Answers

a. Only if state or local law includes pregnancy as a protected class.

Some state and local fair housing laws include pregnancy as a protected class. If they do, then certainly tenants in that state or municipality are protected against discrimination based on the fact that they're pregnant. But because the FHA, which applies across the United States, bans discrimination based on familial status and includes protection against pregnancy discrimination, this answer is incorrect.

b. Because the FHA includes pregnancy as a protected class.

The FHA doesn't include pregnancy as a protected class. But pregnancy is specifically included in the ban on discrimination based on familial status.

d. Only if they already have a child.

The FHA's ban on familial status discrimination protects tenants who are pregnant without regard to whether there are any children under 18 already living in the household.

Question #73:

For a household to be protected against discrimination based on familial status:

a. At least one child in the household must be the parent's biological child.

b. There must be two parents living in the household.

c. There must be two parents living in the household who are married to each other.

d. None of the above.

Hint: The key to familial status is the presence of children.

The correct answer to Question #73 is:

d. None of the above.

Choices a through c are incorrect because they state nonexistent rules regarding parents. For a household to be protected against discrimination based on familial status, the key is that there must be at least one child under 18 years old living in the apartment.

Explanation of Incorrect Answers

a. At least one child in the household must be the parent's biological child.

There is no biological parent requirement when it comes to qualifying for familial status protection. Parents who adopt children have the same housing discrimination rights as people who are the biological parents of their children. Similarly, it makes no difference under the FHA if a child's legal guardian happens to be a blood relative, such as a biological grandparent.

b. There must be two parents living in the household.

Children under 18 may live with just one adult who is their parent or guardian. The FHA's familial status provisions apply the same to a single-parenting situation as it does to a two-parent household.

c. There must be two parents living in the household who are married to each other.

As mentioned above, not only needn't there be two adults living in a household for familial status protection to apply, but the FHA imposes no requirement that two adults be married to each other.

Question #74:

True or false?

Limiting the number of children who may live in an apartment in order to comply with state and local occupancy laws is permissible under the FHA.

The correct answer to Question #74 is:

False.

Explanation: Limiting the number of people who may occupy an apartment may be necessary to meet state or local occupancy requirements. There's no reason to single out children in this context, and doing so could lead to allegations that your policy illegally discriminates based on familial status.

Question #75:

When it comes to sleeping arrangements, a landlord may legally:

a. Require tenants to have their children sleep in separate bedrooms.

b. Bar tenants from sharing their bedroom with a child.

c. Require a family with children to rent a larger apartment than they would like because of local occupancy requirements.

d. Require that only same-sex children sleep in the same bedroom.

Hint: Landlords can't impose their own views of sleeping arrangements that aren't backed by law.

The correct answer to Question #75 is:

c. Require a family with children to rent a larger apartment than they would like because of local occupancy requirements.

A landlord is normally on safe legal ground if local occupancy requirements prevent her from renting a certain size apartment to a family with children. Letting families with children rent apartments that exceed the requirements would require the landlord to violate local law. Also, occupancy requirements exist for a legitimate, nondiscriminatory reason, which is to prevent overcrowding and overtaxing of building systems. HUD's official position since December 18, 1998, based on considerations outlined in an internal memo of March 20, 1991, by General Counsel Frank Keating (known as the "Keating Memo"), is to suggest that, as a general rule, a policy of two persons in a bedroom will be considered reasonable under the FHA. If a landlord adopts a more restrictive policy to comply with state or local occupancy laws, then the landlord is not attempting to violate the FHA's ban on familial status discrimination. In addition to state and local requirements, HUD also considers factors such as apartment and bedroom size, the age of children, and the capacity of septic, sewer, and other building systems in determining fair housing compliance.

Explanation of Incorrect Answers

a. Require tenants to have their children sleep in separate bedrooms.

b. Bar tenants from sharing their bedroom with a child.

d. Require that only same-sex children sleep in the same bedroom.

Landlords can't create rules requiring children to sleep in separate bedrooms, barring parents from sharing their bedroom with a child, or limiting bedroom sharing to same-sex children. Pursuing any of these rules could require tenants to rent an apartment with one more bedroom than they planned, which could be unavailable or beyond their financial reach. As a result, such rules would illegally limit housing choices for tenants because of the fact they have children, in violation of the FHA's ban on discrimination based on familial status.

Question #76:

May landlords legally adopt a rule barring children from displaying rowdy behavior in common areas such as hallways?

a. No, but landlords may adopt a rule barring all tenants from displaying rowdy behavior in the hallways and other common areas.

b. Yes, but only if it's done in response to an existing problem with children acting rowdy in the hallways.

c. Yes, but only if children are defined as being under 18 for purposes of this rule.

d. None of the above.

Hint: Landlords must be sure not to unnecessarily single out children in apartment rules.

The correct answer to Question #76 is:

a. No, but landlords may adopt a rule barring all tenants from displaying rowdy behavior in the hallways and other common areas.

Tenants often complain to their landlord about children who are disturbing them by being loud in the hallway. Very often, this prompts a landlord to adopt a new community rule barring children from displaying rowdy behavior in the hallways and other common areas. There are two problems with such a rule, however. The main problem is that it's illegal because it unfairly singles out children. This means that it imposes a restriction on families with children while not limiting other tenants in the building. The other problem with the rule is that it addresses the narrow issue at hand but doesn't go as far as it should. If banning rowdy behavior in common areas is the goal, then it makes sense to ban all rowdy behavior, without limiting it to a segment of your tenant population, such as children. This way, the rule will be more effective, also covering situations where adult tenants disturb neighbors through rowdy behavior.

Explanation of Incorrect Answers

b. Yes, but only if it's done in response to an existing problem with children acting rowdy in the hallways.

The circumstances leading to the adoption of a rule don't change what's legal. When a landlord seeks to adopt a rule barring rowdy behavior by children in common areas, it's often in response to an ongoing problem with children. The FHA doesn't get in the way of the landlord addressing the problem—it just requires landlords not to single out children when it's not necessary to do so. A rule barring rowdy behavior in common areas (without limiting the rule to children) accomplishes the landlord's goal while also being FHA-compliant.

c. Yes, but only if children are defined as being under 18 for purposes of this rule.

Children are already defined as being under 18 by the FHA in connection with the protection afforded to families with children. As long as children are unnecessarily singled out in a rule, the rule will violate the FHA's ban on familial status discrimination.

d. None of the above.

This choice is incorrect because barring all tenants, and not just children, from displaying rowdy behavior is legal (choice a).

Question #77:

May landlords legally adopt a rule requiring supervision of young children in their apartment community's playground or swimming pool?

a. No, because this would amount to illegal discrimination based on familial status.

b. Yes, because such a rule is aimed at protecting children's health and safety.

c. Yes, but only if all tenants in the apartment community okay this rule.

d. Yes, but only if all tenants with children in the apartment community okay this rule.

*Hint: Landlords may single
out children under certain circumstances.*

The correct answer to Question #77 is:

b. Yes, because such a rule is aimed at protecting children's health and safety.

Normally, singling out children in rules violates the FHA, just as singling out tenants based on their race, religion, or other protected class is illegal. But rules that single out children because they're aimed at protecting children's health and safety are typically legal, because the law recognizes that children have special health and safety issues. So, a rule requiring supervision of young children in an apartment community's playground or swimming pool would be an example of one that a landlord may legally adopt.

Explanation of Incorrect Answers

a. No, because this would amount to illegal discrimination based on familial status.

Just because a rule singles out children doesn't mean it violates the FHA's ban on familial status discrimination. A rule that's aimed at protecting children's health and safety, such as a rule requiring supervision of children in a playground or pool, is legal.

c. Yes, but only if all tenants in the apartment community okay this rule.

d. Yes, but only if all tenants with children in the apartment community okay this rule.

This rule is not an example of illegal housing discrimination because it aims to protect children's health and safety. How much support a rule gets from tenants—either those directly affected by the rule or everyone—has no bearing on whether the rule is in compliance with the FHA.

Question #78:

True or false?

A landlord can point out that an apartment contains uncontrolled lead paint but can't refuse to rent that apartment to a family with children.

The correct answer to Question #78 is:

True.

Explanation: A landlord can certainly point out to a family with children that an apartment contains uncontrolled lead paint. In fact, federal lead paint law requires landlords to make such disclosures. But a landlord can't then refuse to rent an apartment with uncontrolled lead paint to a family with children, even out of sincere concern for the children's health. After making the required disclosure, a landlord must leave the decision to rent that apartment up to the parents (assuming, of course, that the household meets the landlord's tenant selection criteria).

Question #79:

Which of the following isn't accurate regarding apartments with lead paint?

a. Landlords may affirmatively market apartments with controlled lead paint to families with children.

b. Landlords may prioritize addressing lead-paint hazards in apartments with families with children.

c. Landlords may force families with children to permanently vacate their apartment if a lead-paint hazard is discovered.

d. Landlords may require families with children to temporarily live in another apartment while lead-paint hazards are controlled.

Hint: Familial status discrimination is still a concern when lead-paint hazards are discovered.

The correct answer to Question #79 is:

c. Landlords may force families with children to permanently vacate their apartment if a lead-paint hazard is discovered.

Lead paint laws require landlords to inform tenants about possible lead-paint hazards, particularly because of the health risks they pose for young children. However, it's up to each household to decide what to do if a lead-paint hazard is discovered in an apartment. Even if a household includes children, a landlord can't evict the family on account of the hazard.

Explanation of Incorrect Answers

a. Landlords may affirmatively market apartments with controlled lead paint to families with children.

There is nothing preventing landlords from affirmatively marketing apartments with controlled lead paint to families with children.

b. Landlords may prioritize addressing lead-paint hazards in apartments with families with children.

The FHA's ban on familial status discrimination generally means that landlords and other housing professionals can't take action that singles out children. But it's legal to do just that when children's health and safety is at stake. So, landlords may prioritize addressing lead-paint hazards in apartments with families with children without running afoul of the FHA.

d. Landlords may require families with children to temporarily live in another apartment while lead-paint hazards are controlled.

Children's health and safety are threatened when a

lead-paint hazard is discovered, so the FHA doesn't prevent landlords from temporarily relocating families with children to another apartment while working to control known lead-paint hazards.

Question #80:

May landlords legally limit tenancy in a building to singles?

a. Yes, but only if state and local fair housing laws don't ban discrimination based on marital status.

b. No, because the FHA bans discrimination based on marital status.

c. No, because doing so would violate the FHA's ban on discrimination based on familial status.

d. Yes, because the FHA doesn't restrict landlords when it comes to renting to single people.

Hint: Consider what effect such action would have on a tenant's right to avoid discrimination based on familial status.

The correct answer to Question #80 is:

c. No, because doing so would violate the FHA's ban on discrimination based on familial status.

You might think of limiting tenancy in a building to singles as a way of catering to a certain market segment. But while single people may enjoy it, such an arrangement can also be viewed as a way of hurting families with children by limiting their choices in housing. Regardless of the intent, helping singles does also mean hurting families with children because it removes housing options for tenants just because they have children, which violates the FHA's ban on discrimination based on familial status. Also, if a single person residing in a singles-only building wished to have or adopt a child, the landlord's policy would require her to move out.

Explanation of Incorrect Answers

a. Yes, but only if state and local fair housing laws don't ban discrimination based on marital status.

Some state and local fair housing laws ban discrimination based on marital status. If such a law applies, then limiting tenancy in a building to single people would certainly violate that law. But limiting tenancy to singles also violates the FHA's ban on discrimination based on familial status, which is applicable across the United States.

b. No, because the FHA bans discrimination based on marital status.

The FHA doesn't ban discrimination based on marital status. But limiting tenancy in a building to singles violates the FHA's ban on discrimination based on familial status.

d. Yes, because the FHA doesn't restrict landlords
   when it comes to renting to single people.

The FHA doesn't explicitly say that landlords can't rent
to single people, but such a practice would clearly
violate the FHA's ban on discrimination based on
familial status because it limits housing choices for
families with children.

Question #81:

Restricting occupancy of some or all of the apartments in a building to seniors:

a. Can lead to FHA violations if not done properly.

b. Is illegal because the FHA doesn't allow landlords to give preferences.

c. Is legal only if your state and local fair housing laws don't ban discrimination based on age.

d. None of the above.

Hint: The FHA allows exemptions for certain types of senior housing.

The correct answer to Question #81 is:

a. Can lead to FHA violations if not done properly.

If the FHA strictly banned discrimination based on familial status, senior housing as it exists today wouldn't be possible. But under the FHA, landlords may legally refuse to rent to families with children if their buildings qualify under a senior housing exemption. Basically, a building qualifies if either all occupants are at least 62 years old, at least one occupant in 80 percent of the occupied apartments in a building is at least 55 years old, or the building participates in a federal, state, or local senior housing program.

Explanation of Incorrect Answers

b. Is illegal because the FHA doesn't allow landlords to give preferences.

The FHA doesn't allow landlords to give preferences to prospects and tenants based on a protected class. Although familial status is a protected class, landlords who follow the rules for a senior housing exemption may legally give preferences by favoring seniors over families with children.

c. Is legal only if your state and local fair housing laws don't ban discrimination based on age.

The issue with senior housing is whether a landlord can legally turn away families with children. If your state or local fair housing law bans discrimination based on age, such restrictions are enforceable only to the extent they don't conflict with federal law, including the FHA's senior housing exemptions.

d. None of the above.

Landlords who decide to restrict occupancy to seniors can get into fair housing trouble if they don't follow the rules (choice a), so this choice is incorrect.

Question #82:

True or false?

Children might be able to live in a 62-and-older community.

The correct answer to Question #82 is:

False.

<u>Explanation:</u> 62-and-older senior housing requires that every occupant in all apartments is at least 62 years old. So, by definition, children can't live in such a community.

Question #83:

True or false?

Landlords who rent to families with children in a 55-and-older community may still discriminate based on familial status when it comes to the terms and conditions of the rental.

The correct answer to Question #83 is:

True.

Explanation: Just because a landlord chooses to rent to families with children in the 55-and-older type of senior housing doesn't mean the landlord loses the familial status exemption. Landlords in this situation can still discriminate based on familial status when it comes to the terms and conditions of the rental.

Question #84:

Landlords are free to create stricter versions of 55-and-older housing as long as:

a. They apply to HUD for approval of the more restrictive exemption.

b. They don't violate possible state or local fair housing laws that protect against discrimination based on age.

c. They agree not to discriminate based on familial status.

d. None of the above.

Hint: Senior housing exempts landlords from familial status discrimination requirements.

The correct answer to Question #84 is:

b. They don't violate possible state or local fair housing laws that protect against discrimination based on age.

Sometimes, landlords wish to create senior housing that's more restrictive than the 55-and-older program allowed under the FHA. As far as the FHA is concerned, landlords may be more restrictive. However, landlords also need to check that their plans won't violate any state or local fair housing law barring discrimination based on age. To qualify as 55-and-older housing under the FHA, at least 80 percent of occupied apartments in a building must have at least one occupant who's at least 55 years old. If you want to require, for example, all occupants in the 80 percent of apartments to be at least 55 years old, at least one occupant in the 80 percent of apartments to be at least 60 years old (instead of 55), or place an age restriction for the other 20 percent of apartments, you may run afoul of violating age discrimination laws (because the additional self-imposed restriction would require the landlord to turn away prospective tenants based on their age).

Explanation of Incorrect Answers

a. They apply to HUD for approval of the more restrictive exemption.

Landlords who choose to be more restrictive than an exemption requires are fulfilling the requirements of the exemption. So, there's no reason why these landlords would need to seek approval.

c. They agree not to discriminate based on familial status.

Meeting the requirements of a senior housing exemption means not having to comply with the FHA's ban on discrimination based on familial status. Following a stricter version of an exemption is one way to comply with the exemption, so landlords may discriminate against families with children. Also, if landlords wishing to adopt a stricter version of an exemption had to agree not to discriminate based on familial status, they would lose their incentive to follow a senior housing exemption. Plus, in cases where all occupants must be at least a certain age, it would be impossible not to discriminate against families with children while complying with the exemption's requirements.

d. None of the above.

This choice is incorrect because landlords are free to create stricter versions of senior housing requirements as long as they don't violate possible state or local fair housing laws that protect against discrimination based on age (choice b).

Question #85:

Which of the following isn't accurate regarding the 55-and-older senior housing exemption?

a. A landlord must register intent to qualify for this exemption with HUD, and then HUD must certify the property as compliant.

b. A landlord must survey tenants to verify their age at least once every two years.

c. A landlord must publish and adhere to policies and procedures that show an intent to provide housing for people who are 55 and older.

d. A landlord must offer significant services and facilities specifically designed for the property's seniors.

e. a and d.

Hint: Planning to rent to a certain number of tenants 55 and older and actually doing so is key.

The correct answer to Question #85 is:

e. a and d.

Each of these statements inaccurately describes a landlord's responsibilities when trying to comply with the 55-and-older senior housing exemption.

Explanation of Incorrect Answers

a. A landlord must register intent to qualify for this exemption with HUD, and then HUD must certify the property as compliant.

This is inaccurate because the FHA imposes no such requirement. However, landlords should check if state or local laws require them to register intent to provide senior housing.

b. A landlord must survey tenants to verify their age at least once every two years.

The FHA requires landlords to perform age verification every two years for as long as they wish their property to continue qualifying under the 55-and-older senior housing exemption.

c. A landlord must publish and adhere to policies and procedures that show an intent to provide housing for people who are 55 and older.

Landlords must communicate the fact they are seeking the 55-and-older senior housing exemption when talking with prospects, advertising vacancies, and through other means. This requirement is intended to help prevent landlords from claiming they were trying to comply with this exemption as a defense to a fair housing complaint based on familial status.

d. A landlord must offer significant services and facilities specifically designed for the property's seniors.

This requirement was removed by the Housing for Older Persons Act (HOPA), which took effect on December 28, 1995.

Question #86:

True or false?

If a household includes adult children who live with their parents, they're not covered under the FHA's ban on discrimination based on familial status.

The correct answer to Question #86 is:

True.

Explanation: The FHA's ban on familial status refers to the presence of at least one child under 18 years old. Once every child in a household turns 18 and becomes an adult, familial status protection is no longer available.

Question #87:

True or false?

The FHA requires landlords to rent to a family with children with poor credit before renting to two adult roommates with excellent credit.

The correct answer to Question #87 is:

False.

Explanation: The FHA requires landlords only to avoid discriminating against prospects and tenants just because they have children. If a landlord requires tenants to have excellent credit, she may legally reject applications from tenants with poor credit, regardless of the fact that they may have children.

Question #88:

For a person to be protected by the FHA based on disability, which of the following must be true?

a. The person's disability must fit the FHA's definition.

b. The person must be declared "disabled" by a licensed physician.

c. The person must reasonably and sincerely believe that he has a disability.

d. All of the above.

Hint: The FHA has a specific, objective definition of disability.

The correct answer to Question #88 is:

a. The person's disability must fit the FHA's definition.

For someone to qualify for protection under a law, that person typically must meet certain requirements as set up by that law. This is the case with qualifying for protection against disability discrimination under the FHA. The FHA defines disability (calling it "handicap") broadly, to include any impairment that "substantially limits" one or more "major life activities."

Explanation of Incorrect Answers

b. The person must be declared "disabled" by a licensed physician.

If a person fits the FHA's definition of disability, then he qualifies for the protection that this law affords. Just because a physician may believe that a person is "disabled" doesn't mean he's eligible for the FHA's protection. What matters in this context is whether the person has a disability as the FHA defines it.

c. The person must reasonably and sincerely believe that he has a disability.

Tenants and prospective tenants don't get to decide that they're eligible for protection against disability discrimination under the FHA based on their own definition or concept of the term. (Neither do landlords and property managers, for that matter.) The relevant inquiry here is only whether a person fits the FHA's definition of disability. Finally, it's possible that a tenant with a mental illness that fits the definition of disability reasonably and sincerely (yet inaccurately) believes he doesn't have a disability.

d. All of the above.

Fitting the FHA's definition of disability is the only one of the choices that's a requirement for qualifying for protection against disability discrimination. So, this answer is incorrect.

Question #89:

True or false?

Only disabilities involving physical limitations qualify for protection under the FHA.

The correct answer to Question #89 is:

False.

Explanation: The FHA specifically defines disability to include a "physical or mental impairment."

Question #90:

True or false?

A landlord may reject an applicant with a mental illness who is dangerous or poses a threat to others.

The correct answer to Question #90 is:

True.

Explanation: A mental illness qualifies as a disability under the FHA. But landlords may reject applicants or take action against tenants who pose a "direct threat to the health or safety of other individuals or whose tenancy would result in substantial physical damage to the property of others"—regardless of whether they have a mental illness.

Question #91:

To be protected against disability discrimination under the FHA, a tenant's disability:

a. Must be obvious.

b. Needn't be obvious but must be demonstrated in some way to the landlord.

c. Needn't be obvious but must substantially limit a major life activity.

d. Must be obvious or require the tenant to use an assistive device.

Hint: The only relevant inquiry is whether the tenant's disability fits the FHA's definition.

The correct answer to Question #91 is:

c. Needn't be obvious but must substantially limit a major life activity.

One of the key characteristics of a disability under the FHA is it must "substantially limit a major life activity," such as breathing, walking, eating, talking, thinking, and sitting. Not only is there no requirement that the disability be obvious, but many disabilities that fit the FHA's definition aren't obvious.

Explanation of Incorrect Answers

a. Must be obvious.

b. Needn't be obvious but must be demonstrated in some way to the landlord.

d. Must be obvious or require the tenant to use an assistive device.

The FHA doesn't give landlords the right to be convinced of a tenant's disability through personal observation. So, as mentioned above, the FHA doesn't require a disability to be obvious to qualify for protection against discrimination. Also, if a tenant's disability isn't obvious to a landlord, the tenant needn't demonstrate or explain the disability in any way. Finally, a tenant doesn't have to rely on the use of a cane, wheelchair, hearing aid, or other assistive device to be protected.

Question #92:

Which of the following qualifies as a disability under the FHA?

a. An addiction to illegal drugs.

b. HIV/AIDS.

c. Asthma.

d. Alzheimer's disease.

e. All of the above.

f. None of the above.

Hint: The FHA defines disability broadly.

The correct answer to Question #92 is:

e. All of the above.

The FHA defines disability broadly. Each choice is considered a disability under the FHA, and so a tenant or prospect who has the condition or disease mentioned would be protected against housing discrimination based on a disability.

Explanation of Incorrect Answers

a. An addiction to illegal drugs.

An addiction qualifies as a disability because it's an impairment that substantially limits one or more major life activities. The fact that a prospect's or tenant's addiction is to illegal drugs doesn't void the FHA's protection.

b. HIV/AIDS.

HUD regulations specifically note that HIV and AIDS are examples of disabilities, and so discrimination against people because they have either one is illegal under the FHA.

c. Asthma.

Many people who have asthma are able to control it with preventative or rescue inhalers and other medication. But prospects and tenants who are asthmatic are protected against disability discrimination even if their asthma is under control or rarely triggered.

d. Alzheimer's disease.

Alzheimer's disease substantially limits major life activities. As the disease progresses, a tenant may acquire the need for additional reasonable accommodations.

f. None of the above.

This answer is incorrect because each one of the choices listed qualifies as a disability under the FHA.

Question #93:

True or false?

Landlords can legally refuse to rent to tenants with HIV or AIDS out of health and safety concerns.

The correct answer to Question #93 is:

False.

Explanation: HIV and AIDS aren't spread through casual contact, and tenants who have HIV or AIDS are protected by the FHA's ban on discrimination based on disability. So, landlords can't cite health and safety concerns to legally turn away tenants because they have HIV or AIDS.

Question #94:

A landlord may charge a pet deposit for a service animal if:

a. The landlord charges pet deposits for all animals in the building.

b. The landlord charges less of a deposit for service animals than for pets.

c. The landlord contributes half of the deposit for a service animal.

d. None of the above.

Hint: Service animals,
which are needed for a
disability, aren't considered pets.

The correct answer to Question #94 is:

d. None of the above.

A landlord may not charge a pet deposit for a service animal because doing so requires the tenant to pay for having a disability. Tenants with service animals need them as a reasonable accommodation for a disability. For example, a guide dog may help a visually impaired tenant get around the building. Or a cat may give emotional support to a tenant who suffers from severe depression. By contrast, tenants keep pets for companionship and enjoyment. Landlords who charge tenants a pet deposit must limit the deposit to pets.

Explanation of Incorrect Answers

a. The landlord charges pet deposits for all animals in the building.

Very often, landlords get into fair housing trouble because they don't take the same action with all tenants. This answer might seem correct because the landlord appears to be treating everyone the same. But here, the landlord is treating tenants the same as other tenants who aren't similarly situated. When it comes to tenants with disabilities, landlords often must take different actions to ensure they're treating them fairly. Tenants who have a dog, cat, or other animal as a reasonable accommodation for a disability don't have a pet that would be subject to a landlord's pet deposit. Such animals are service animals that tenants need for a disability, so requiring tenants to pay for them is disability discrimination.

b. The landlord charges less of a deposit for service animals than for pets.

Charging a lower amount of a security deposit isn't

compliant with fair housing law because you're still treating the animal as a pet and still charging the tenant to have what amounts to a reasonable accommodation for a disability.

c. The landlord contributes half of the deposit.

This is similar to choice b, and is essentially saying that tenants with disabilities must pay half of what others pay for a pet deposit. As just mentioned above, charging any amount for a reasonable accommodation for a disability violates the FHA's ban on disability discrimination because it requires tenants to pay simply for having a disability.

Question #95:

Which of the following actions would violate the FHA?

a. Charging a pet deposit for a service animal.

b. Requiring that a tenant pay more of a security deposit because he uses a wheelchair.

c. Requiring that a tenant get insurance relating to her use of a motorized wheelchair.

d. All of the above.

Hint: Requiring tenants to pay
for having a disability violates the FHA.

The correct answer to Question #95 is:

d. All of the above.

Renting to people with disabilities but making them pay extra in some way because of the fact that they have a disability violates the FHA.

Explanation of Incorrect Answers

a. Charging a pet deposit for a service animal.

Service animals are needed as a reasonable accommodation for a disability. So, although a landlord may charge a pet deposit to tenants who wish to keep pets in their apartment, landlords mustn't charge this deposit to tenants who need a service animal.

b. Requiring that a tenant pay more of a security deposit because he uses a wheelchair.

Landlords who are concerned that wheelchairs may cause damage can't require tenants to pay a higher security deposit. Tenants may be liable to their landlord for damages to their apartment beyond reasonable wear and tear, which could be caused by a wheelchair. But making tenants set aside money to cover potential damage from a wheelchair would violate the FHA's ban on disability discrimination.

c. Requiring that a tenant get insurance relating to her use of a motorized wheelchair.

Tenants who use a motorized wheelchair need to do so on account of a mobility impairment. Just as with the example of an increased security deposit (as discussed above), requiring insurance (which requires payments in anticipation of potential damage from a motorized wheelchair) means discriminating based on disability.

Question #96:

Which of the following doesn't the FHA protect?

a. Alcoholism.

b. An addiction to legal drugs.

c. An addiction to illegal drugs.

d. The use of illegal drugs.

e. All of the above.

*Hint: An activity isn't
the same thing as a protected
disability, even if it's related to a disability.*

The correct answer to Question #96 is:

d. The use of illegal drugs.

The FHA protects prospects and tenants based on certain characteristics they may have. The use of illegal drugs isn't a characteristic but an activity. So, for example, if a tenant is arrested for using illegal drugs at an apartment community and the landlord wishes to evict him because his action is a material violation of the lease, the tenant can't use the FHA to argue he's protected against the eviction.

Explanation of Incorrect Answers

a. Alcoholism.

Alcoholism is a disease involving addiction to alcohol, and so people who are alcoholic have a qualifying disability under the FHA.

b. An addiction to legal drugs.

c. An addiction to illegal drugs.

People who are addicted to drugs are protected against housing discrimination for their addiction because of the FHA's ban on disability discrimination. It doesn't matter if the drug that a person is addicted to is legal.

e. All of the above.

This answer is incorrect because the use of illegal drugs (choice d) is the only choice that refers to an activity (which isn't protected), as opposed to a characteristic.

Question #97:

If a prospect tells a landlord that she has a disability, which of the following is now true?

a. The landlord has violated the FHA's ban on disability discrimination.

b. The landlord is entitled to follow up with questions about the nature or extent of her disability.

c. The landlord has the right to get assurances from the prospect that she would be able to live independently at the building.

d. The landlord will violate the FHA by discussing the prospect's disability only if she's a minority.

e. None of the above.

Hint: If a prospect chooses to offer unsolicited information about a disability, it doesn't change anyone's rights or responsibilities under the law.

The correct answer to Question #97 is:

e. None of the above.

This choice is correct because each of the other listed choices involves an inaccurate account of how the FHA works.

Explanation of Incorrect Answers

a. The landlord has violated the FHA's ban on disability discrimination.

You can't control what prospects choose to tell you without prompting from you. So, simply being told by a prospect that she has a disability involves no discrimination on your part and isn't actionable.

b. You're entitled to follow up with questions about the nature or extent of her disability.

The FHA regulations generally bar landlords from inquiring into the "nature or severity" of a prospect's or tenant's disability. If a prospect volunteers information about the fact she has a disability, it doesn't waive this protection or change the law.

c. The landlord has the right to get assurances from the prospect that she would be able to live independently at the building.

Asking a prospect for assurances that she'll be able to live independently at your building requires you to solicit information about the nature and extent of her disability, including her medical history, which is illegal. Even if the impetus behind such questions is a desire to help, it's important to let all prospects decide what help they need and arrange for that help on their own.

d. The landlord will violate the FHA by discussing the prospect's disability only if she's a minority.

This choice is incorrect because one discrimination ban based on a protected class doesn't depend on another. In this case, if you've violated the FHA, it's because of the prospect's disability—regardless of her race. A further discriminatory action based on a prospect's race would mean an additional violation.

Question #98:

If a landlord notices that a prospective tenant uses a wheelchair, the landlord may:

a. Assume she's interested in one of the building's accessible apartments.

b. Assume she wants to rent a ground-floor apartment.

c. Ask the prospective tenant if she's interested in an accessible or ground-floor apartment.

d. None of the above.

Hint: Acting based on good intentions doesn't necessarily lead to fair housing compliance.

The correct answer to Question #98 is:

d. None of the above.

A landlord who sees a prospective tenant using a wheelchair might be tempted to assume she wants an accessible or ground-floor apartment, or at least ask. But this sort of response, even though it may be fueled by a desire to help, can lead to fair housing trouble.

Explanation of Incorrect Answers

a. Assume she's interested in one of the building's accessible apartments.

b. Assume she wants to rent a ground-floor apartment.

Each of these choices is incorrect because it involves a landlord who's making assumptions about a prospective tenant's housing needs based on a perceived disability.

c. Ask the prospective tenant if she's interested in an accessible or ground-floor apartment.

Although this choice doesn't involve assumptions, the landlord is still asking for fair housing trouble because he's treating a prospective tenant differently based on a perceived disability. Prospects who want to limit their apartment search to a certain floor or type of apartment can express their needs on their own, if they so choose. If landlords wish to make sure prospects know about accessible apartments, they should ask all prospects, on applications and guest cards, if they're interested in an accessible apartment.

Question #99:

True or false?

Landlords can limit the number of tenants who use wheelchairs if there's a concern that the apartment community will resemble a hospital or nursing home.

The correct answer to Question #99 is:

False.

Explanation: Some landlords don't wish to rent to tenants who use wheelchairs because they're concerned about the image of their building, fearing that it will resemble a hospital or nursing home. Since the FHA bans discrimination based on disability, such concerns have no legal merit. Tenants who use wheelchairs need them for a disability, and that need trumps any concern a landlord may have about how his building might come across to others.

Question #100:

Is a tenant who has albinism protected under the FHA?

a. No, because the FHA doesn't include albinism as a protected class.

b. Yes, if the tenant is discriminated against based on color or disability.

c. No, because albinism isn't listed as a qualifying disability.

d. Yes, because the FHA specifically bans discrimination against people with albinism.

*Hint: The FHA doesn't offer
a definitive list of qualifying disabilities.*

The correct answer to Question #100 is:

b. Yes, if the tenant is discriminated against based on color or disability.

Albinism isn't a protected class under the FHA, nor is the word "albino" mentioned anywhere in the law. But a tenant with albinism may bring a claim under the FHA against a landlord or other housing professional if the tenant believes she was discriminated against based on color or disability related to albinism.

Explanation of Incorrect Answers

a. No, because the FHA doesn't include albinism as a protected class.

This choice speaks to an important principle, which is that just because something isn't listed as a protected class or identified elsewhere in the FHA doesn't mean there's no related protection under the FHA. Tenants with albinism could pursue a fair housing claim against a landlord for discriminating against them based on color and disability.

c. No, because albinism isn't listed as a qualifying disability.

The FHA doesn't offer a list of conditions, diseases, and impairments that qualify for protection against disability discrimination, and the regulations only list examples. Instead, the FHA requires that a prospect's or tenant's condition, disease, or impairment fit the definition of disability to qualify for protection.

d. Yes, because the FHA specifically bans discrimination against people with albinism.

As mentioned, the FHA doesn't need to specifically ban

discrimination against a condition, disease, or impairment for it to qualify for protection. The FHA protects against disabilities that include an impairment that "substantially limits" one or more "major life activities."

Fair Housing Helper for Apartment Professionals

Question #101:

Which of the following statements is accurate about service animals under the FHA?

a. The FHA limits service animals to dogs.

b. The FHA limits service animals to dogs with special training.

c. The FHA limits service animals to dogs plus other types of animals that have special training.

d. The FHA doesn't limit service animals to dogs or have any special training requirements.

*Hint: Service animals need
to help a tenant in some way
in connection with a disability.*

The correct answer to Question #101 is:

d. The FHA doesn't limit service animals to dogs or have any special training requirements.

Letting a tenant with a disability keep a service animal is an example of a reasonable accommodation under the FHA. The FHA doesn't specifically mention service animals, and therefore it doesn't limit service animals to dogs or animals with special training. The issue of service animals arises when a prospect or tenant needs to keep an animal in connection with a disability but the landlord refuses, citing a no-pets rule. In this case, the prospect or tenant may be entitled to a reasonable accommodation. If a request to have a particular animal passes muster under the FHA as a reasonable accommodation—it's needed for a disability and wouldn't impose a substantial administrative and financial burden—then it should be granted.

Explanation of Incorrect Answers

a. The FHA limits service animals to dogs.

b. The FHA limits service animals to dogs with special training.

c. The FHA limits service animals to dogs plus other types of animals that have special training.

The FHA places no limits on service animals. To keep one as a reasonable accommodation for a disability, a tenant must show that the particular animal is needed in connection with her disability and that keeping the animal in her apartment wouldn't impose an undue financial and administrative burden on the landlord.

Question #102:

True or false?

Landlords must allow all tenants in the building to keep pets in their apartment if at least one tenant needs a service animal to accommodate a disability.

The correct answer to Question #102 is:

False.

Explanation: This isn't a situation where if you make an exception for one tenant, you must make it for all. In this case, a tenant is keeping a service animal as a reasonable accommodation for a disability, which is part of how the FHA protects tenants with disabilities. Other tenants who wish to keep pets simply for companionship and enjoyment, and not in connection with any disability, may be limited by a landlord's no-pets rule.

Question #103:

True or false?

If a landlord must grant a tenant's request to keep a service animal as a reasonable accommodation for a disability, then the landlord is barred from applying any pet rules to that tenant's service animal.

The correct answer to Question #103 is:

False.

<u>Explanation:</u> If you allow pets at your community, there's a good chance you require tenants to follow basic rules aimed at protecting health and safety. For example, many landlords include a pet addendum in their leases requiring pets to be spayed or neutered, dogs to be leashed in common areas, and tenants to clean up after their pets and take their pets for regular vet visits and get any required vaccinations. You can apply the same rules to any tenants who keep a service animal in their apartment. Similarly, if you don't allow pets but let a tenant keep an animal as a reasonable accommodation for a disability, you can create these types of rules to apply to this tenant.

Question #104:

True or false?

If a request for a reasonable accommodation or modification isn't in writing, a landlord isn't required to consider it.

The correct answer to Question #104 is:

False.

<u>Explanation:</u> The FHA doesn't require requests for reasonable accommodations and modifications to be made in writing, and HUD and the DOJ made clear in guidance that landlords must consider all such requests, regardless of whether they're in writing.

Question #105:

To request a reasonable accommodation for a disability, a tenant must:

a. Put the request in writing.

b. Personally make the request.

c. Follow the step-by-step procedure as outlined in the FHA.

d. Specifically indicate that the tenant is requesting a "reasonable accommodation."

e. All of the above.

f. None of the above.

Hint: Tenants who don't follow formalities may still be entitled to accommodations.

The correct answer to Question #105 is:

f. None of the above.

In a memo, HUD and the DOJ clarified that tenants seeking a reasonable accommodation for a disability needn't follow special procedures. Not only does this make it easy for tenants to request accommodations they need, but it prevents landlords from hiding behind a technicality either in the law or in their internal procedures to shield them from improperly denying a reasonable accommodation request.

Explanation of Incorrect Answers

a. Put the request in writing.

Making a request in writing is a good idea for a few reasons. It helps ensure a tenant is clearly conveying the message he intends, the written message itself is proof of the request and when it was made, and the writing adds a level of formality to the request, which helps show the tenant is serious about it. All that said, a landlord cannot insist that accommodation requests be made in writing. If a tenant verbally requests an accommodation, the landlord must consider it just as if it had been made in writing. Of course, landlords who are frustrated by verbal requests may wish to put them in writing themselves.

b. Personally make the request.

If a prospect or tenant needs an accommodation for a disability but doesn't personally make the request, a landlord can't ignore or deny the request for this reason. Also, landlords can't ask tenants why they can't make the request in a certain manner, as this may be related to their disability. Tenants needn't follow any formality such as personally visiting the landlord or contacting her by phone, and it's okay for a family member, friend, or other representative of a tenant to make the request on the tenant's behalf.

c. Follow the step-by-step procedure as outlined in the FHA.

The FHA doesn't include step-by-step procedures for making reasonable accommodation requests. Once a prospect or tenant makes a request, the landlord must consider it and then grant the request, if reasonable.

d. Specifically indicate that the tenant is requesting a "reasonable accommodation."

Prospects and tenants can't get penalized for not properly labeling their request as one of reasonable accommodation. If, for some reason, a request is unintelligible or it's just not clear to a landlord that the request is for a reasonable accommodation, the landlord may ask for clarification.

e. All of the above.

None of the choices listed is correct (choice f), so all of the above is incorrect.

Question #106:

Which of the following is true about landlords and reasonable accommodation requests from tenants with disabilities?

a. Landlords must anticipate such requests and grant them.

b. Landlords must anticipate such requests but only grant them if a tenant confirms that they're needed.

c. Landlords mustn't anticipate such requests.

d. Landlords mustn't anticipate such requests, unless a tenant's disability is obvious.

Hint: Anticipating reasonable accommodation requests can backfire.

The correct answer to Question #106 is:

c. Landlords mustn't anticipate such requests.

The FHA imposes no affirmative responsibility on landlords to anticipate tenants' possible reasonable accommodation requests. Not only would doing so be impractical or impossible in many cases, but it would likely lead to fair housing violations. For this reason, a landlord's job is to take all accommodation requests from tenants seriously and grant them, if reasonable. If a tenant believes he needs an accommodation, it's up to the tenant to initiate a request for one.

Explanation of Incorrect Answers

a. Landlords must anticipate such requests and grant them.

Landlords aren't tasked with being mind readers, and so, as explained above, they're not required to anticipate tenants' possible needs based on a disability. Moreover, landlords who attempt to do so (for example, by approaching only tenants who use a wheelchair or who have an obvious or noticeable disability) are treating tenants differently based on a disability, which violates the FHA.

b. Landlords must anticipate such requests but only grant them if a tenant confirms that they're needed.

Presumably, landlords who anticipate requests would grant them only if tenants confirm they're actually needed. But landlords who anticipate accommodation requests are violating the FHA.

d. Landlords mustn't anticipate such requests, unless a tenant's disability is obvious.

Even if a tenant's disability is obvious to a landlord, anticipating such a tenant's accommodation request still violates the FHA's ban on disability discrimination. Also, some tenants with non-obvious disabilities may need an accommodation while other tenants with obvious disabilities don't.

Question #107:

True or false?

If a landlord lets a tenant have a full-time or part-time live-in aide as a reasonable accommodation for a disability, then the landlord may need to grant additional accommodations.

The correct answer to Question #107 is:

True.

<u>Explanation:</u> Depending on community rules, a landlord may need to make additional accommodations so that a tenant's live-in aide can do her job and provide the needed assistance to the tenant. For example, if the aide will drive the tenant around in her car, then the landlord may need to grant the aide permission to park in the community's lot, even if it's normally limited to tenants. The same would hold true for using tenant-only laundry facilities.

Question #108:

When a tenant makes an accommodation request, the landlord:

a. Must consider it carefully.

b. May ask for backup from the tenant's physician confirming the need for the request.

c. May deny the request if granting it would impose an undue financial and administrative burden.

d. Should suggest reasonable alternatives to unreasonable requests.

e. All of the above.

Hint: Properly handling accommodation requests means taking them seriously.

The correct answer to Question #108 is:

e. All of the above.

Each of the options listed applies when a tenant makes an accommodation request. Most importantly, landlords must consider accommodation requests carefully so that they can grant them, if reasonable. Although asking questions about the nature or severity of a tenant's disability can lead to fair housing trouble, landlords shouldn't be afraid to ask for backup in the form of a letter from the tenant's physician (or other appropriate third party) confirming the need for the accommodation request. Landlords needn't grant every request—just the ones that are reasonable. To be reasonable, granting a request mustn't impose an undue financial and administrative burden on the landlord's operations. Finally, if a landlord believes that a tenant's accommodation request is unreasonable, the landlord should, if possible, suggest alternatives that would be reasonable.

Explanation of Incorrect Answers

a. Must consider it carefully.

b. May ask for backup from the tenant's physician confirming the need for the request.

c. May deny the request if granting it would impose an undue financial and administrative burden.

d. Should suggest reasonable alternatives to unreasonable requests.

After a tenant makes an accommodation request, each one of the options above applies, and so the correct answer is all of the above (choice e).

Question #109:

Which of the following is accurate regarding who pays for reasonable modifications?

a. Tenants are always responsible for the cost of reasonable modifications.

b. Landlords are always responsible for the cost of reasonable modifications.

c. Tenants generally must pay for their cost, unless your apartment community gets federal assistance.

d. You generally must pay for their cost, unless your apartment community gets federal assistance.

e. None of the above.

Hint: Allowing a modification usually doesn't mean paying for it.

The correct answer to Question #109 is:

c. Tenants generally must pay for their cost, unless your apartment community gets federal assistance.

Landlords are required to consider all modification requests (such as a ramp or bathroom grab bars) and grant them if they're reasonable. But they're normally not required to pay for creating the modification. There's an exception, however, if an apartment community gets federal assistance, in which case the landlord is responsible for the cost.

Explanation of Incorrect Answers

a. Tenants are always responsible for the cost of reasonable modifications.

b. Landlords are always responsible for the cost of reasonable modifications.

d. You generally must pay for their cost, unless your apartment community gets federal assistance.

e. None of the above.

These choices are incorrect because, with the exception of an apartment community that gets federal assistance, tenants who get a landlord's permission to make a reasonable modification must pay for its cost.

Question #110:

Which of the following statements is accurate regarding who must maintain reasonable modifications in working order?

a. Tenants are always responsible for the upkeep of reasonable modifications.

b. Landlords are always responsible for the upkeep of reasonable modifications.

c. A tenant is responsible for maintaining a modification in working order if it's used exclusively by that tenant.

d. Landlords are responsible for maintaining a modification if it's located in part of the common area that's normally maintained by the landlord.

e. c and d.

Hint: The location of a modification is a determining factor.

The correct answer to Question #110 is:

e. c and d.

HUD and the DOJ issued guidance on reasonable modifications, making it clear who's responsible to maintain physical modifications. If a modification (such as a ramp) is used only by the tenant who requested it, then the tenant is responsible for keeping it in good working order. As for common area modifications, tenants are only responsible for their upkeep if they're in a part of the common area that the landlord doesn't normally maintain.

Explanation of Incorrect Answers

a. Tenants are always responsible for the upkeep of reasonable modifications.

b. Landlords are always responsible for the upkeep of reasonable modifications.

c. A tenant is responsible for maintaining a modification in working order if it's used exclusively by that tenant.

d. Landlords are responsible for maintaining a modification if it's located in part of the common area that's normally maintained by the landlord.

These choices are incorrect because they are too general (choices a and b) or are only part of the correct answer (choices c and d).

Question #111:

True or false?

Landlords can require tenants to restore reasonable modifications that were made to common areas or building exteriors.

The correct answer to Question #111 is:

False.

Explanation: Under the FHA, landlords may require tenants to restore modifications made only to the inside of their apartment at the end of their tenancy.

Question #112:

True or false?

If a multifamily building was built for first occupancy after March 13, 1991, it must be in compliance with certain design and construction requirements.

The correct answer to Question #112 is:

True.

Explanation: Multifamily buildings (with four or more apartments) that were occupied after March 13, 1991, as well as those buildings where the last building permit or permit renewal was issued after June 15, 1990, are required to have been built in compliance with the FHA's design and construction requirements (following one of the several HUD-approved safe harbors for compliance). The purpose of this law is to ensure that such buildings are accessible and usable by people with disabilities. If your building doesn't have an elevator, only the ground-floor apartments are covered by the requirements. The FHA's seven design and construction requirements are: 1) an accessible building entrance on an accessible route, 2) accessible common and public use areas, 3) doors that are usable by people who use a wheelchair, 4) an accessible route into and through an apartment, 5) light switches, electrical outlets, thermostats, and other environmental controls placed in accessible locations, 6) reinforced bathroom walls for possible later installation of grab bars, and 7) kitchens and bathrooms that are maneuverable by people who use a wheelchair.

Question #113:

True or false?

Whether or not a building must comply with the FHA's design and construction requirements, the landlord may need to provide a designated parking spot for a tenant with a disability.

The correct answer to Question #113 is:

True.

Explanation: If the FHA's design and construction requirements apply to your building, then at least two percent of the number of parking spaces serving apartments covered by the requirements must be made accessible and located on an accessible route. Also, even if the requirements don't apply, landlords must consider tenants' requests for parking spaces that are needed as a reasonable accommodation for a disability.

Question #114:

True or false?

Landlords shouldn't consider tenants' apartment transfer requests if they're not related to a disability.

The correct answer to Question #114 is:

False.

Explanation: The FHA requires landlords to consider reasonable accommodation requests, such as a request to transfer to a different apartment, if tenants need them because of a disability. But there's no reason landlords can't consider and grant transfer requests from tenants who wish to move for other reasons, such as to obtain more space, a lower rent, or a better view. If you let tenants make transfer requests for any reason, keep good records of how you handle each request so you have proof that you acted in a fair, nondiscriminatory way.

Question #115:

If a tenant doesn't have a disability, then the FHA's ban on disability discrimination may protect that tenant if:

a. The tenant lives with someone who has a disability.

b. The tenant has visitors who have a disability.

c. The tenant once had or was misclassified as having a disability.

d. The landlord mistakenly believes the tenant has a disability.

e. All of the above.

f. None of the above.

Hint: There are ways tenants may be discriminated against based on disability even if they don't have a disability.

The correct answer to Question #115 is:

e. All of the above.

Short of actually having a disability, there are other ways a tenant may be protected against disability discrimination under the FHA. A tenant who lives with someone who has a disability may be adversely affected if a landlord or other housing professional limits that person's housing choices. A tenant may also have a claim under the FHA if he has visitors who have a disability. For example, there have been cases involving landlords who don't like renting to people who use wheelchairs because they claim to be concerned that their property will resemble a nursing home. If a landlord expresses disapproval to a tenant for having guests over who use a wheelchair, this is also a violation.

Explanation of Incorrect Answers

a. The tenant lives with someone who has a disability.

b. The tenant has visitors who have a disability.

c. The tenant once had or was misclassified as having a disability.

d. The landlord mistakenly believes the tenant has a disability.

Each one of these choices shows how tenants without a disability are protected against discrimination based on disability, so all of the above (choice e) is correct.

f. None of the above.

Each one of the choices listed is correct (choice e), so none of the above is incorrect.

Question #116:

True or false?

Parts of an apartment community that are open to the public, such as an on-site rental office, must be accessible for people with disabilities, even if the FHA doesn't apply.

The correct answer to Question #116 is:

True.

Explanation: Rental offices and other areas that are open to the public are covered by Title III of the Americans with Disabilities Act of 1990 (ADA). The ADA requires that such areas remain accessible for people with disabilities.

Question #117:

True or false?

A landlord's policy of allowing tenants to keep pets except for certain dog breeds is discriminatory and therefore a violation of the FHA.

The correct answer to Question #117 is:

False.

Explanation: The FHA doesn't protect pets against discrimination (based on breed or any other factor). Also, if a landlord doesn't allow a breed because of her insurance company and a prospect happens to request to keep a dog of that breed as an accommodation for a disability, such a request would likely not be considered reasonable because it would impose an undue financial and administrative burden on the landlord (who needs the insurance for her business). In this situation, the landlord should suggest choosing a different breed as a reasonable alternative.

Next Steps

Congratulations!

Now that you've completed the Quiz, you should have a greater understanding of fair housing law and what you need to do to achieve compliance.

Remember, fair housing compliance isn't just about avoiding violations. Your efforts also boost your professional reputation and go a long way toward maintaining good tenant relations.

Follow the instructions on the next page to confirm your status as a FairHousingHelper.com Gold Professional and enjoy the benefits.

You've earned it.

FairHousingHelper.com
Gold Professional

Follow these easy instructions:

1) Visit **www.fairhousinghelper.com/nextsteps.html**

2) Enter your name and contact information.

   Please note that Fair Housing Helper respects your privacy as much as you do. Rest assured your information will be kept strictly private and will not be shared or sold to any third party.

3) Confirm your purchase of this book and completion of the Quiz, then click Submit.

4) Congratulations! You're a **FairHousingHelper.com Gold Professional**...

   You can now:

   ➡ Expect a welcome e-mail that includes:

   ✓ a badge to put on your Web site and marketing materials as evidence of your training and to show your commitment to fair housing compliance, and

   ✓ instructions for obtaining a free personalized Certificate of Training that you can print and hang on your office wall.

   ➡ Stay informed about new developments that affect your business, and be the first to learn of new Fair Housing Helper products and updates.

Fair housing compliance is an essential part of lowering your risk as a housing professional...

but it's not the end of the story.

Every Landlord's Property Protection Guide
10 Ways to Cut Your Risk Now

by Ron Leshnower
Published by Nolo ℘ Print (with CD) or eBook

ISBN-13: 978-1-4133-0700-9
ISBN-10: 1-4133-0700-0

AN AMAZON.COM #1 MULTI-CATEGORY BESTSELLER

---

helps you identify common risky situations and get specific, practical advice for dealing with them.

....

"Leshnower draws upon his years of experience and expertise to provide a month-by-month plan that can be adopted and customized by any landlord for any property so as to avoid damaging lawsuits while protecting their financial investment both short-term and long-term."

—*Midwest Book Review*

....

VISIT **RONLESHNOWER.COM** FOR MORE INFORMATION

22651590R00163

Made in the USA
Lexington, KY
07 May 2013